Where Are You From

Where Are You From

Letters to My Son

Tomás Q. Morín

University of Nebraska Press   Lincoln

Publication of this volume was assisted by
the School of Humanities and the Office
of Research at Rice University.

Acknowledgments for the use of copyrighted
material appear on pages 117–18, which
constitute an extension of the copyright page.

The University of Nebraska Press is part of a land-
grant institution with campuses and programs on the
past, present, and future homelands of the Pawnee,
Ponca, Otoe-Missouria, Omaha, Dakota, Lakota, Kaw,
Cheyenne, and Arapaho Peoples, as well as those of the
relocated Ho-Chunk, Sac and Fox, and Iowa Peoples.

♾

Library of Congress Cataloging-in-Publication Data
Names: Morín, Tomás Q., author.
Title: Where are you from : letters
to my son / Tomás Q. Morín.
Description: Lincoln : University
of Nebraska Press, 2024.
Identifiers: LCCN 2023038642
ISBN 9781496237767 (trade paperback)
ISBN 9781496239433 (epub)
ISBN 9781496239440 (pdf)
Subjects: LCSH: Morín, Tomás Q.,—Correspondence. |
Authors, American—21st century—Correspondence. |
Fathers and sons—United States. | BISAC: LITERARY
COLLECTIONS / Letters | SOCIAL SCIENCE / Ethnic
Studies / American / Hispanic American Studies
Classification: LCC PS3613.O7542 Z486
2024 | DDC 811/.6—dc23/eng/2023
LC record available at https://lccn.loc.gov/2023038642

Designed and set in Chaparral Pro by L. Welch.

For Rebecca,
Chloe, and Boomer

Contents

Where Are You From

Letter from a Sub-Sub-Basement

My son,

I am a man uneven. My right shoulder drops. A grin shows my teeth don't line up. One ear is higher than the other. And my foot, my left foot . . . I should start with my toes. There are blisters and they hurt. There's a story there. My left foot is wider than the right. Not by much, mind you. But enough. (And the right foot is longer than the left!) Come look if you don't believe me. Now, I'm not a freak, some mismatched toy of God. No one would ever know any of this if I didn't tell them. The naked eye hasn't been made that could tell the difference between my feet. Not even an eye wearing clothes could do it.

How do I know? I sold shoes once upon a time. During the holidays. We had a tool called the Brannock Device. I didn't know that's what it was called, though. It was invented in the '20s. Should I say 1920s? Maybe I should. You'll start high school in 2033, and so the 2020s will be closest to you.

But toes!

I was going to tell you a story about toes. I hope you have your mother's pinky toes. Like a compass needle, they point true north. Carrying a baby loosens the ligaments of a mother's feet.

Find your mother and massage her feet.

And do it often.

I have my father's toes. Your tío Juan does too. We also have our father's hands. My index and pinky fingers curve inward. So do my pinky and big toes. We humans were fish once. You can see it in the shape of my flippers. If I wear the wrong shoes and walk too much, the inside of my tucked pinky toes will blister.

I have stepped on myself all of my life. If we have the same feet, then that will surely be part of your inheritance.

You've seen me grouchy. A blister is an expressway to grouchy. My patience grows small and hides from me.

In Texas I've never worried about feeling this way. But here in New Jersey, it's another story. And not just New Jersey. People like us . . . brown, brown people I mean . . . we've been shot, strangled, tazed, lynched, and beaten while living happily. Grouchy is almost an invitation to be snuffed out. So I'm trying to be careful here in Madison because, well, I want to meet you. If I survive the next sixteen weeks, then I can do that.

The first time I walked to Stop & Shop for groceries, the sun was high. I thought a marvelous mile of bright light would cure my homesickness. I had not met you yet, but I had, really.

Who says meeting can only happen in the air after all?

I knew your mother's belly, and so I knew you even if you did not yet know me.

I digress, but you already know this; you know me to be a lover of tangents, a tangent machine. You also know that I don't love them for their own sake. I'm not one of those simple fools who babble on and on and never get to the point; by now you know me and thus have seen that I always circle back around. How could I not? To do otherwise would be to court the unevenness I loathe, the very one that lives in my body. Symmetry is my king and queen. An open circle is no circle; it is merely a letter C that has lost its way.

Okay, I was walking. You love clothes, as your mother and I do, and if we did anything right, then you do as well, so I will tell you what I was wearing: gray fleece shorts (with three pockets—always buy them with three pockets), a light blue tank top, and my light blue denim Toms shoes. Toms says they are gray, but I know blue when I see it. If you don't believe me, check the closet because I probably still have them. I take care of what I love. Your tío Juan was the opposite when we were kids. Our abuelo called him "lumbre." It means "fire." I wonder how hot you will burn. I'm fire too, but I smolder low and long. So I was walking and had left the edge of campus behind. So far, so good. There were trees and cars, even a bird singing. I had no reason to expect the day would carry anything strange. You would think forty-plus years of living in the South would have taught me better. It didn't.

I passed a bookstore, Thai and Greek restaurants, a wine store. It was Anytown, USA. People sat at benches and tables enjoying their lunch. I brushed off the first person that stared at me for too long as an aberration. The same with the second. By the fourth and the fifth, I knew I was not on the receiving end of a seemingly endless string of unfortunate coincidences. A part of me wanted to believe that I was, though. That is what this country does to you; it makes you think that what is real and obvious in front of you could not be so. It starts when you're young. Ask your tío Juan if he remembers when he was a little boy and I punched him in the face with his own fist and said, *Stop hitting yourself. Why are you hitting yourself?* People will tell us, *Stop being paranoid. You see racism everywhere. Give people a chance.* If they ever tell you that, mijo, tell them my favorite line from *The Outlaw Josey Wales*: "Don't piss down my back and tell me it's rainin'."

The men looked at me as if they had seen my face on a wanted poster. The women stared at me like you would at a dog with muddy paws that just ran in the house. There was an old woman who I thought was going to fall over. She was short, so she kept leaning her head back and back to take in the totality of my body. Her eyes were like coasters. I bet you her neck hurt for days. When her masseuse asked her how she hurt her neck, I wonder if she was honest and said what she was really thinking: *I was staring at this giant beaner in town.* In Texas I am an invisible man. In this tiny town of northern New Jersey, I am anything but when people wonder where I am from.

In the state of my birth—the one into which you, too, will greet the day with a cry that announces, *I am here!*—it is easy to blend in when it seems like almost every other person looks like you. I don't even have to try to be invisible. My side of the family has been in Texas since at least the 1700s, long before there were United States north of the Rio Grande. This reminds me of a story James Baldwin told in 1969. He was visiting the West Indian Student Centre in London. When you read this, put this book down and find me so we can watch it together. But just in case the revolution has intensified, the one against us that would see us all in the grave or in chains, the one that would erase our memories of what it means to be human and treated with respect, then maybe the video won't exist anymore. Or maybe my memory will be shot, and I will have faded into senility early. We should prepare for both, so I will set down Baldwin's story for you here:

> Many years ago when I first came to London, I was in the British Museum, naturally. [*Laughter.*] And, uh, one of the West Indians who worked there started up a conversation with me and wanted to know where I was from. And I told him I was from Harlem. And that answer didn't satisfy him. And I didn't understand what he meant. "I was born in Harlem. I was born in Harlem hospital," I said. "I was born in New York." None of these answers satisfied him.
> He said, "Where was your mother born?"
> And I said, "She was born in Maryland." And I could see, though I didn't understand it, that he was growing more and more disgusted with me. He became more and more impatient.
> "Where was your father born?"

"My father was born in New Orleans."

"Yes," he said, "but, man, where were you born?"

And I began to get it, you know, well, I said, "My mother was born in Maryland, my father was born in New Orleans, I was born in New York."

He said, "But before that, where were you born?" [*Laughter.*]

And I had to say, "I don't know." And I could see that he did not believe me. I tried to explain, "You know, um, there's no way for me to—"

He said, "Don't you care enough to find out?"

And I tried to explain that if I were originally from Dakar or from wherever I was in Africa, I couldn't find out where it was because my entry into America is a bill of sale. And that stops, you know, that stops you from going any further.

I always think of this story when someone asks me, *Where are you from?* True, true, I've been asked that question in many states, but never as much as in New Jersey. Some days that question comes twice. I always say, *From Texas.* They then ask, *Where were you born?* because, you see, I could mean that I lived in Texas or grew up there, but really I was born somewhere else. When I tell them I was born in Texas, they then ask, *Where are your parents from?* Again I say, *Texas.* Puzzled, a few people then confidently ask, sure that they now have in their possession the correct question by which they can determine my . . . my what exactly? *When did your family come to Texas?* they finally ask. This is the point, my son, when on a good day, a day like today when I've awoken with the chorus of "Oh Happy Day" in my head for no reason at all, on a day like this I will smile and say, *My family came to Texas before there was a United States. We never crossed the border; the border crossed us.*

What is it they're after? What is the knowledge they so desperately dig for, and what would they do with it once they secured it?

My son, we are lucky in that we don't have a bill of sale blocking our family history. Unlike Baldwin and so many African Americans, there is a paper trail we can follow that will lead us back to Spain, to the land from which our people crossed an ocean to come here to these continents to steal, murder, and enslave. To become rich. No, to become richer. The paper trail of our history may be crinkled from centuries of age, but it is stiff with the blood of millions.

Once, a fellow professor from Cuba asked me these questions. His parents were from Cuba. Another time it was a student from Costa Rica. They were trying to find commonality, I'm sure. And I was not trying to be flip. Anything but. But for everyone else, I think, maybe (and this is my nature as an optimist showing here) they want an entry into a conversation about immigration, about how our government's vile immigration policies are affecting me and my own. In decades past, conversations about ancestry were about people building family trees to see when and where their family came to this continent from France or Ireland or Russia. But now one's very right to stay in this country, the very country of their birth, is being brought into question. The attack from those who hate any brown person who looks "Mexican" is fierce.

If a brown family crosses the southern border into the United States without documentation, their children are stripped from them. Thousands of these children have been flung across the country into the foster care system like trash thrown out the back door. A heinous and un-Christian act if ever there was one. President Trump has shouted that we need a wall to protect us against the murderers, rapists, and gang members he says are assaulting the border daily. Now there's something new, something we feared, or should have—the stripping of citizenship from anyone born here who looks "Mexican." Birth certificates are undergoing unfair scrutiny even as I write this now. The government has even asked one man to produce his family's Bible as evidence to prove what he has known his whole life, that he is a citizen of these United States.

I always think that these times in which I write you could not be any more absurd. But then I think, of course they could. After most of the "Mexicans" were deported, next would be African Americans. I'm sure on some racist agenda in a smoky back room, somewhere on their list they have reinstituting Jim Crow, then re-enslaving every Black person they can't kill or send back to Africa. While racist America is using deportation against us, it has made a special whip for African Americans: police violence. We, too, have heard its snap. Their plan is simple: the police will kill and terrorize African Americans, and Immigration and Customs Enforcement (ICE) will terrorize and deport Latinos.

Your mother just asked me if my experience with racism here in Madison has been different from my experience with racism in Texas. I could not have said *yes!* faster if I had tried. I told her that my time here has taught me something I had always suspected to be true, even though I never had proof of it: like Baskin-Robbins, racism comes in thirty-one different flavors. All my life I had known one bitter flavor, a flavor that had ceased to be bitter, in fact, because I had tasted it for so long. If the hatred here tastes bitter, then it is only because this flavor had been unknown to me.

You're paranoid . . . you're a sick man . . . you hate white people! This is what my accusers would say to me if they had the courage, my son. One may do it too. And what should I say back? If I said, *No, I'm a visible man*, they would be confused. If I said, *I could never hate you more than you hate yourself*, they might be tempted to lay hands on me. And what would I do then? The measure of my response would depend on if it was a blister day or not. You thought I had forgotten about toes, didn't you? I may be a lopsided man, but I meant it when I said I wouldn't make these letters to you a sea of *CCCCC*s.

I wonder every day how visible you will be, my son. Will you wear the light skin of your mother's family from Wales and England? Or the light skin of my mother that came from her mother's family by way of Spain and the Canary Islands? Or will your little bones be draped in my skin and my father's skin that was even darker than my own? People will say you are *half and half*, but you're not milk. DNA doesn't work that way. Racism even less so. People will either see you as friend or foe.

How will I guide you if you can pass for an enemy? How can I teach you to decide whether to stay quiet or reveal yourself when someone who hates us takes you into their confidence with words about *beaners*, *spics*, and *wetbacks*? You could punch them in the mouth and preserve the wholeness of your spirit that they would devour one bloody bite at a time. You could do that. Or you could say nothing and stay safe on the outside as they chew your spirit and pass it through each of their six stomachs until it's just a mash of self-loathing.

I don't know what to tell you, mijo.

I have never experienced this because I have never looked like anything other than what I am. Maybe try to remember that the root of all this hate is not a race problem; it's a fear problem. They fear us because they think we would take away their power and then treat them just as they have treated all people of color. You can't convince the racist otherwise. Even their little ones.

I walked to the Stop & Shop again today. I didn't want to because my toes were blistered, but I needed food. So I grabbed my cart and started with the side of the store closest to the doors and then proceeded to work my way to the other end because only a maniac would flit around from aisle to aisle like a bee with no apparent sense of order; a maniac, I am not. What's more, I'm in hostile territory, and so one needs to always have a plan and be efficient when one is behind enemy lines. Apples, lunch meat, salad, chips; a fifth of the store is done. Bread, soups, pasta, pesto. Raisins . . . now I wander, looking for raisins when it happens. I make the turn from one aisle into another, and a little white girl of about ten years of age—the age of your big sister right now—this little girl, she sees me, her eyes widen, and she grabs her father's leg in terror, and they then begin to walk as if they were contestants in a three-legged sack race on the Fourth of July.

Sometimes, my son, sometimes not even words are needed, sometimes the blunt teeth of their little ones are enough to tear off a chunk of your soul. She and her father walked on as I walked past them. Seventy years ago I might have had my head staved in because of this child's fear. Seventy years might seem like a long time, but it isn't. My mother, your abuela, is seventy-two. Only two years before she was born, the Supreme Court ruled segregation was unconstitutional in *Brown v. Board of Education*. One year later Emmett Till, a boy from Chicago visiting family in Mississippi, was kidnapped, beaten, shot in the head, and thrown into a river. Why? They said he flirted with a white woman. Decades after her husband and his brother had been found not guilty by a white jury, she said she made it up.

Someone who was alive then might tell me, *You survived! No one even called you a spic! That's progress!* And they would be right; it is progress. But when I think of the scar on my spirit left by that little girl's face, I know this progress isn't enough. When I told this story to my friend Vievee (she's like a sister and cried when I told her you would be coming into the world; she can't wait to meet you), we talked about how all the people of color in Madison are mostly workers. I suppose the figure I strike—without an apron or a uniform or a weed eater in my hand—must be an odd one to the residents of Madison. As Vievee said, *They don't have any experience with a brown man of leisure.*

I think she's right about that, even if we can't see into the souls of all these people I have crossed paths with, unlike you, whose skin is just leaving its translucence behind. Today is the second ultrasound I've missed, and I'm heartbroken. Your mother sent me pictures of the last one. I could see your tiny bones through your skin. She said you sucked your thumb the whole time, except once when you pulled it out, blew a kiss, and then commenced to suck it again. I hope that charm keeps you safe and takes you far.

After the incident with the little girl, I thought long and hard about how to return hostile stares in the future. A smile isn't just for pleasantries, my son; it can be a weapon too, just like a machete belongs both to revolutions and the farm.

When they stare at me, I want my smile to tell them that I know why they are staring, and what's more, I think they're fools because of it. *But what about staying safe?* you think. We've made progress, my son! Moreover, harvest is good for the soul, even if it means that all that cutting down dulls the blade of my smile. It's okay because I can re-sharpen it by doing things that make me happy like eating good food, running my hand along the bark of a tree, playing basketball, reading, watching superhero movies, buying a comic, and yes, eating cake.

Never forget that we are beautiful. But don't fold this knowledge into a square and hide it in your pocket; you can lose it in the wash that way. Raise that head high and wear it on your body, carry it in the shine of your teeth, in the stillness of your eyes, from up in the curls of your hair down to the soles of your feet.

A file and toenail clippers will do in a pinch. But a sanding stone is best. What were once blisters a few days ago have dried and hardened. The calluses are streaked with old blood inside. My sanding stone is back home with your mama and sister. I don't even have a proper file, just that metal one attached to the clippers. It'll have to do. I lift one foot up to my knee, then the other. I cut the rough skin with the clippers, careful not to cut soft skin. I try to smooth the jagged skin that's left with the metal file. The world has tried to harden me at every turn, just as it will to you. Resist it for as long as you can. And when you feel yourself failing, ask for help. You are not alone. None of us are, even if at times we feel like it.

That we feel alone is not an accident; it's a calculated effect of the system of racism in this country. The more we feel the oppression we wrestle against is our individual burden, the greater the chance it will crush us. Plantation owners enslaved Africans from tribes that spoke different languages for a reason. Racists become uncomfortable when they hear us speaking Spanish for a reason.

Sonsofbitches . . . speak English . . . sneaky fucks . . . go back to your country. They think this. Don't believe me? Read their faces. Every word is there "written not in Spanish, not in Greek, not in Latin, not in shorthand but in plain American which cats and dogs can read!" Wait, is that right? Maybe Marianne Moore said, "in plain Hate which cats and dogs can read!" Does it matter? Probably not. Dogs and cats can read both anyhow. They fear we are plotting against them (racists, not dogs and cats), laying the groundwork for the revolution that is to come.

Maybe we are. And maybe we are trading the recipes our abuelas gave us for enchiladas. Or maybe we are strategizing for getting out the vote. Either way, a threat is a threat is a threat, as Gertrude Stein once put it. They don't ban Spanish in the schools anymore like they did when your abuela went to school. Just like news of the end of the Civil War was slow to reach Texas, so was desegregation of Texas schools. Your abuela sat in a classroom with all the other children who looked like her. The white kids had their own building. And the African American kids were in their own as well. Theirs was closest to the cotton gin, so when they came out of the building, they were covered in ash.

We are always in their periphery, seen but unseen. When you lift your head from this book and look around, what do you see? What are the faces like, O boy of the future?

What do those faces see when they see you?

When they see us walking together?

When I walk you to school, do they think I'm your grandfather?

Or do they think I'm the landscaper doing my boss a solid by walking his son to school?

How many times have people come up to you and asked, *Do you know this man? Is this man bothering you?*

I wish I could press my lips to your mother's belly and whisper to you the words with which to answer these people, but I cannot. I will not. My voice today, this voice from the past, this voice will not serve you. If I try to cast my voice right now into the future, to make it vault off this page and into your throat so that you could speak my rage and indignation, my voice would crumble to nothing and float away on the wind. My voice is of my time, and your voice will be of a different time. Even so, I live in your throat and in your lips, flesh of our flesh. You must find your own indignation. Don't worry, the world will give you plenty of opportunities to sharpen your smile. When you speak, I will speak with you. In your voice will be the echo of my life.

In what language do I live? I live in none. I live in you. It is your voice that I begin to hear and it has no language. I hear the motions of a spirit and the sound of what is secret becomes, for me, a voice that is your voice speaking in my ear. It is a misery unheard of to know the secret has no name, no language I can learn.

Mark Strand wrote that in *The Monument*. Do you recognize it? You should. Your mother is reading it to your sister right now. And I have been reading it to you since before you could talk. A future boy must know about time if he is going to travel it. In that paragraph Strand is talking to his translator in the future. Since I am talking to you that must mean you are my translator. Not the translator of my words, but the translator of my body and the body of your mother. Even before your skin kissed the air for the first time, you were in your mama's belly working away on your first book.

What kind of a translator will you be? Will you be one of those sad literalists obsessed with matching word with word? Or will you be wild and reckless like Robert Lowell in his *Imitations*? While I hate Rilke (maybe that's too strong. Loathe. That's it—I loathe most of Rilke's poetry), I love Gass's *Reading Rilke*, and it makes me think of you and the care with which your tiny baby bones are forming behind invisible skin that will be invisible no more and the flame in your eyes and the . . . I'm rambling now, so here's some Gass on Rilke and translation to shut my trap.

> Tone, too, is a very tricky thing. Recently Anita Barrows and Joanna Macy translated Rilke's *Book of Hours* for Riverhead Books. Here is a sample. The poet is presumably addressing his god, but we know the divinity in question is actually Rilke's quondam lover, Lou Salomé.
>
> > Extinguish my eyes, I'll go on seeing you.
> > Seal my ears, I'll go on hearing you.
> > And without feet I can make my way to you,
> > without a mouth I can swear your name.
> >
> > Break off my arms, I'll take hold of you
> > with my heart as with a hand.
> > Stop my heart, and my brain will start to beat.
> > And if you consume my brain with fire,
> > I'll feel you burn in every drop of my blood.
>
> I feel that the tone of my version is fiercer, more ardent, but it is perhaps more a love poem now than a religious one.
>
> > Put my eyes out: I can still see;
> > slam my ears shut: I can still hear,
> > walk without feet to where you were,

and, tongueless, speak you into being.
Snap off my arms: I'll hold you hard
in my heart's longing like a fist;
halt that, my brain will do its beating,
and if you set this mind of mine aflame,
then on my blood I'll carry you away.

What a sordid business this eye gouging and snapping of arms. The only thing worse than a hopeless romantic is a violent romantic.

Don't let the deranged masochists and sadists fool you, my son. Pain is not the path to love; love is the path to love. But tone is of the utmost importance! You are a work of art, but you are not alone on your canvas. Lie on your back, my boy, and what I know will be plain as day to anyone who looks at you from the side; the paint of your canvas is ten feet thick. Under your paint are your mother and me. And under us are the sketches of both our lines that stretch into the past for thousands of years. I can hear you laughing and thinking, *Who's the romantic now?* But do you know what lives in my cheek? One swab and I discovered that I have 287 Neanderthal variants in my DNA. That's 68 percent more than the millions of others who were tested. Our family cave is a fine and distinguished one, so be kind and fair, O child translator of the future. My father? Yes, I count his voice too. I tried to forget it. For good reason. It's best for me not to speak about him on an empty stomach. Practice your math until I return. Two times two is five, and so on . . .

Where was I? Oh yes, fifteen years . . . for fifteen years my father and I didn't speak. That's not right. For fifteen years I chose not to speak to my father. That's better.

In his poem "September 1, 1939," W. H. Auden wrote, "We must love one another or die." He was young. People love that line. Auden didn't. After he sent the poem into the world, he realized that the line was bullshit. We all die whether we love each other or not. Once, he reprinted the poem but changed the line to "We must love one another and die." That's not much better because it states the obvious. He knew it too, so he eventually stopped reprinting the poem. For fifteen years with your grandfather I practiced, "We must not love one another and die." And so he did. But before that day a few months ago, I wrote a poem that was about him and not about him.

CARITÀ AMERICANA

I found regret in a deli case;
it was white and shaped like a brick.
On the label a cow from Vermont
grazed on forget-me-nots or drank
from a pond. I can't remember which,
since it was the black splatters
—or was it white splotches—
I was taken with, and the thin legs,
and the elegant body shaped like a tank.
Although, what I remember most
is the missing udder, that pink fist
of gravity every Holstein swings,
whose absence could have been intended
because the artist hoped liberating his cows
from the bondage of breasts
(an act of charity, no doubt,
though not Roman; Hindu, maybe)
would impress the feminist he was dating
who was head over heels
for vegan babka.

The meat cutter offered me a taste,
because he saw how I kept staring
longingly in his case (as if I were starving)

at that blessèd cow without nipples
drawn by a lovesick artist in Jersey
who wanted me to believe it gave the milk
that made the immaculate cheese
now sitting in my hand,
whose taste I already knew well,
even though I played the naïf, even though
I knew better, that after I had chewed the last bite
of that sacred square, in two minutes time,
maybe less, I would begin expanding,
but not with the Holy Ghost,
with lactose, in the small intestine,
so that by the time I reached my car
I'd be ready for the fiddle
because I would look like one of the demented
Roman emperors, the ones that were all paunch
and wild eyes and who had a taste for fire.

To the young meat cutter waiting
for my answer, for 5 o'clock, for an escape
from the madness of fluorescent lighting,
I wanted to say Thou, wanted to be formal,
not because it rhymed with cow,
it was that magical beast after all that joined us,
but because we were beyond the quotidian now,
and biblical time is archaic
and thus it would only be proper to say, "Thou
slicer, Thou priest of the cold cut
who set me on the path
of suffering with an act of charity,
do you know your Vermeer, your Caravaggio
and Rubens, and thus the story
of Pero and Cimon, and how the one,

the grown child, fed the other,
her jailed father, in secret, with the milk
of her body, so that he wouldn't die
as had been decreed, from want, from lack
of food and drink,
and how when all was discovered
the father was released and the daughter's gift
was named Carità Romana?"

I mumble, "Thou, Thou," and then,
"No, thanks," because I'm already late
to visit my father in the hospital,
in his cold room which, in another country,
one thick with forests and secrets,
with caves to hide in from the authorities,
would be for enemies of the state.
He's a prisoner of his body
—his hunger is vulgar, beastly even,
but unlike Pero, there is no milk in my chest,
which I would let him cleave and suckle anyway
but for the bitterness swimming there.
He looks almost Roman now
with his buzzed head and marching veins.
For all his brio, he'll never teach another son
how to steal corn by moonlight,
just enough to eat and sell,
or how to build a house, or how to read
the soot marks on any brick
from the great Chicago fire of 1871.

When he wakes and adds his lowing
baritone to the shrieks and trills
of his neighbors down the hall,
I clear my throat and do my best cowbird

and watch his face cloud
with yearning, a naked shyness,
like the kind a calf wears
when it's startled by your voice
and it drops its mother's nipple to stare at you,
milk still hot on its tongue.
His sweet cow face is almost enough
for me to forget the old injuries,
how he laughed every time I wretched
in the bathroom because of the butter
he hid in my food. No, I can't lie
and tell him what he wants to hear,
will not say that I love him, will not
admit to that. Instead, I'll wash his hair
and clip his nails, shave his face,
and when my traitorous lip trembles
with pity, I'll whistle
louder, longer, and teach him about regret,
feed it to him one note at a time,
and though he knows he shouldn't,
he'll devour it with the knowledge
that my song will swell and split his heart.

When the Romans sentence Cimon to death by starvation, his daughter Pero asks to visit her father in his last days. When it's discovered that she has been feeding him from her breast, they are not fed to the lions or bears or nailed to crosses as you might expect. Quite the contrary, Cimon is set free because the Romans have been so moved by the beautiful and unexpected love of his daughter.

They called it charity, but it is love.

While writing my poem I imagined my father dying, the father who had been dying in my memory since the day he left our home when I was ten years old, that man, that man who I loved and was lost to me, I put a version of him and a version of me in a hospital room in order to play out his end of days. Why? To imagine the death of someone I loved dearly was a way I had grieved since I was a child like you. It was like pre-grieving. Maybe a part of me always knew that I needed to get a head start on the loss that might spin me out of control. Or maybe I just have a sick mind. Would I even know it if I did?

Unlike in the poem, when the last day came, the real life me didn't find the words *I love you* hard to say at all. In fact, I found myself saying them instantly and with all my heart as soon as we were reunited. Instead, there were three other words that snuck up on me. These three words had been hiding themselves deep within the forest of my heart. No, my son, in the final hours there was no hospital, only his bed at home.

We sat there and watched his body breathe in and out. In and out. That was all it could now do. His mouth was open and his eyes were closed. His wide chest, the chest I had long ago yearned so dearly to lay my head on, rose and fell like a great bellow on a cold fire. His wife said I should talk to him because the nurse had said he could hear us. I leaned in close to that body from which my body had come and stroked his hair. His forehead felt cold to my lips. I don't know why, but I could not stay and watch his last breath. So I kissed him one last time, said *I love you*, and then whispered *I forgive you*. And then I was gone.

I hadn't planned on writing to you about my father. It had been over a week since I had last sat down to write you. I kept clearing the decks and clearing the decks and then nada, zip, zilch. I couldn't. I wanted to but couldn't. I was telling your mother about it tonight, and there is something deep in my spirit that is reluctant to return to writing to you about my time here in Madison. Describing for you how people treat me in town empties the well of strength I draw upon to survive living in this place where a person of color is so unwanted. I told your mother that if I were writing this a year from now and I lived somewhere else, then the time and space would give me the shield I need to wander back into my life here. But instead I am doing it now because I fear that if I don't, then you might never know what I know.

To live it and then to write about it in real time is a double wound.

If my well of strength and hope empties, then I fear what might happen the next time I walk to town to fetch groceries. If I say something in my defense, then the police could be called on me. And for a man who looks like me, mijo, well, in Madison that could mean I would leave this world before you ever entered it.

I know what you're thinking, that despair has infected my spirit. But that's not true! Hope lives in my body and in my spirit such as it can. I'm filled with love and am happy with my life. But this country, this country tries to crush us at every turn. To preserve the strength of my spirit and my body—the spirit has to live some-place—I am not going to write you the series of diary entries that line up with each of the weeks you have left in your mother's belly. Instead, I'll pour everything this country is showing me into these letters as fast as I can.

My grandfather, my mother's father, was one of those people that believed tomorrow was promised to no one. When he woke, he was grateful for having done so. He would rise and make the sign of the cross toward each corner of his room. Or maybe he did this before he went to bed. No matter. The lesson is the same: gratitude.

What did I eat when I stepped away for lunch? I'm not sure why you'd want to know, but I had a sandwich. The bread was Mike's Good Bread, which for some reason I keep calling Dave's Good Bread. It was the seeded one that looks like it was blasted by a shotgun full of seeds. Between the slices I spread honey ham, spicy mustard, and pickles. Lime tortilla chips on the side. If you take after both your mother and me, then you won't tolerate lactose. Don't stand for it! Do you have any idea what lactose does to people like us when we take it into our bodies?

It rots.

Just sits in your gut and rots while your stomach, confused and at a loss of what to do with such a wretched thing, contracts and contracts until eventually the lactose makes its way through you. Don't treat your body like a trash can. I say this knowing full well that I had a slice of swiss on my chicken sandwich today. In my defense, however, swiss is easier to digest, at least for me, than other sources of lactose. If the lactose eaters have tried to shame you for not being able to digest lactose, remind them that digesting lactose is a mutation and that they are the freaks. Our guts are just as nature intended them. Digesting lactose is surely one of the marks of the children of capitalism.

You think I've gone off the deep end, don't you?

It's simple: the mutation for adults digesting lactose didn't exist in the human body 20,000 years ago. And then it did. Why? No one knows for sure, but communities becoming less nomadic, disease, and the nutrient richness of milk no doubt contributed to its prevalence. Even so, only about 35 percent of adults in the world have the lactase enzyme to digest lactose-rich foods. Join us in rebuking the vile substance. And don't fret about not being able to eat ice cream because we'll take you for the best ice cream in the world, coconut ash. It's gray and has the flavor of a thousand beach fires lit under a full moon. You will love it.

Food is a welcome distraction. I eat when I'm sad. Like lactose, racism sits in my body. But unlike lactose, nothing at the pharmacy can help. If the capitalists could create, mass-produce, and sell a little pill to the public that would help us cope with the sorrows of racism, then they surely would. Oh, wait—cocaine, alcohol, crack, cigarettes, LSD, sugar, weed . . . and on and on. If only the cost of these were as small as lactose packets.

I spent last weekend with you and your mother. You have been growing inside her for twenty-seven weeks now. The doctor said you are just fine. But your poor mother—you are separating the muscles of her belly. They say after you are born, physical therapy should help her get back to normal. Those are the doctor's words, not mine. You are not even here yet, and I already know that normal is on a scale and that the scale slides to a new position when a child enters your life. Am I being too literal? Am I overanalyzing everything? You sound like your tío Juan. He used to say that to me all the time when we were kids.

I thought when I returned to Texas that I would enjoy being invisible again. I was wrong. I was so very wrong. In Texas, I was never an invisible man. Sure, I blended in among everyone else who looked like me. But that did not mean that I was unseen. On the contrary, I was seen in Texas. When your mother and I ran errands in town, people saw me for what I am, a human being. Moreover, a man, a partner, a soon-to-be father. I had not been able to appreciate this before living in a place where I felt like a piece of livestock that had found a weak spot in the fence and escaped. When those who curse my very existence see people like me, it's as if they are staring into the sun, the very sun that gives life to this ball of mud we call home.

Which Frenchman said, "Property is theft"? I forget. Property and theft are the twin pillars of these United States. The response to the genocide of North American Indigenous tribes and the horror inflicted upon African slaves and their descendants has been a collective *Oops*.

Women in this country couldn't even vote until 1920. That must seem like so far in the past for you. Your abuela's mother was nine years old in 1920. The Civil Rights Act was passed in 1964. You probably think, *But that was so long ago too!* Your abuela was eighteen years old when this country finally put on paper that it is illegal to discriminate against someone based on their race, color, religion, sex, or national origin. That was only twelve years before I was born.

Our country was pulled kicking and screaming into the language of equality. The most recent example of all this is today's announcement that a group of senators is pushing forward the nomination of Judge Brett Kavanaugh. By the time you're reading this will anyone remember the courage it took Dr. Christine Blasey Ford to testify about how Kavanaugh sexually assaulted her when they were in high school? Does anyone remember Anita Hill's courage? I have no doubt the dishonest bully Kavanaugh will be someone you know because his fingerprints will be on decisions that will affect us all for generations to come. Never forget the lessons on kindness and respect your mother and I have taught you. Be a blinding light in the face of hate and power.

The reality of equality has been something different. And thus the resentment has had generations to fester. When I returned to New Jersey from Texas, I was sad. While at the grocery store in Madison, I was drawn to the muffin case. I was bent over trying to read the labels, salivating over the red velvet muffin that was no doubt ribboned with that vile lactose when I stood up and locked eyes with a child. I'd guess she was twelve or so. She was running toward the muffin case when our eyes locked, her face froze, and like a cartoon character about to run off the side of a cliff, she slammed on the brakes. She stared at me for a moment, then turned around and bolted back to her mother who was at the deli. I sighed. How could I not when the incident was already making my stomach churn? If this hadn't happened, if she had kept running toward the muffin case for the treat she was after, I probably would not have bought a muffin and skipped the discomfort. But my stomach was already knotted, so what difference would it make? Chocolate, I chose a double chocolate one because if I'm going to feel like hell, I might as well taste heaven on the way down.

I was vegan once. Have I told you that? Twice, actually. *Wait, why? How?* you ask. Last week a student came to my office. She looked around at the wire bristle tchotchkes of mice and beavers on my shelves . . . the ant with a hoe made from wire . . . the two rhinos . . . elephant bookends ridden by stoic monkeys . . . the metal butterfly made from a sparkplug . . . my bear who has turned his back on autumn . . . the picture of ants walking on yellow glass . . . the mini donkeys crowned by noon light . . . and the picture of Elizabeth Bishop in Brazil holding her cat Tobias . . . the student looked and looked and said, "Why do you have all these animals in your office?"

"Because I love animals," I said. She smiled.

The simplest answer is sometimes the happiest answer, you know? That was the same reason why I became vegan. I didn't want to eat suffering with two sides of regret at every meal. There is so much pain in the world. Is industrial pain worse, the kind where a culture becomes a machine of death? Is this worse than the random pain and shock that comes for a chicken snapped on the family farm? I don't know. Some cultures believe animals are our brothers and sisters, that we live neither above nor below them but alongside. Think of our sweet pup Boomer. Does he not see you as his little brother even though you are now taller and bigger than him? Never forget how he guarded you even when you were still inside your mama's belly.

All my life I was taught to kill a fly when I saw one. I never questioned this. And then one summer I noticed a fly at the back door trying to get out. I opened the door and tried to shoo it out, but it seemed scared and kept bumping against the glass. I said, *Let me help you. I promise I won't hurt you*, and stretched one finger out like an olive branch. A finger branch! To my delight the fly jumped on my finger and let me give it a ride around the door and outside. This scene repeated itself many times that summer. Flies even let me gently pick them up by a wing when they were too scared to jump on my finger.

People said the flies must be drunk on insecticide, but I never thought so. I think they heard the kindness in my voice, the same tone I've used when we tuck you in at night. Did I ever tell you someone once called me "the Animal Poet"? You know that poem "Woodchucks" by Maxine Kumin I don't like reading? It's not because it's a bad poem. On the contrary, it's powerful. Its power overwhelms me. The poem is a box filled with hard truths about us humans that I know too well.

WOODCHUCKS

Gassing the woodchucks didn't turn out right.
The knockout bomb from the Feed and Grain Exchange
was featured as merciful, quick at the bone
and the case we had against them was airtight,
both exits shoehorned shut with puddingstone,
but they had a sub-sub-basement out of range.

Next morning they turned up again, no worse
for the cyanide than we for our cigarettes
and state-store Scotch, all of us up to scratch.
They brought down the marigolds as a matter of course
and then took over the vegetable patch
nipping the broccoli shoots, beheading the carrots.

The food from our mouths, I said, righteously thrilling
to the feel of the .22, the bullets' neat noses.
I, a lapsed pacifist fallen from grace
puffed with Darwinian pieties for killing,
now drew a bead on the little woodchuck's face.
He died down in the everbearing roses.

Ten minutes later I dropped the mother. She
flipflopped in the air and fell, her needle teeth

still hooked in a leaf of early swiss chard.
Another baby next. O one-two-three
the murderer inside me rose up hard,
the hawkeye killer came on stage forthwith.

There's one chuck left. Old wily fellow, he keeps
me cocked and ready day after day after day.
All night I hunt his humped-up form. I dream
I sight along the barrel in my sleep.
If only they'd all consented to die unseen
gassed underground the quiet Nazi way.

I'm sure someone called Kumin "the Animal Poet" at least once
in her life. I have felt the murderer rise up hard in me a couple of
times like Kumin. I can hear you now: *But, Dad, you said the speaker
isn't always the poet!* True, true, son, true. But before Kumin read
this poem at the Guggenheim Museum in 1979, she said, "This is
a terribly autobiographical poem." Unlike Kumin, I like to hide my
voice behind the masks of speakers whose shoulders don't drop,
who have straight teeth and toes and perfectly balanced ears. It's
the hearts of my speakers that are asymmetrical; they have spirits that have been bent so long they don't remember what it was
ever like to point true north. The compass in their chest always
points to pain.

Does your frown mean you think I've gone overboard again?

I know, I know, I've always had a fondness for the absolutes:
never, always, forever, etc. Where was I? Rage! Murder! Yes, don't
do it. Unless your life is in danger, of course. Or mine. Or your
mother's or sister's. No leaf of swiss chard is worth taking a life for
Christ's sake. Count to ten. Take a walk. Call me or your mother
or your sister if you ever feel like killing someone.

Don't be like the foul specimens who stab me with their mur-
derous eyes here in Madison. If it were up to them, they'd just as
soon display me in a magic show on their festival days. I can see

it now: *Come one, come all, to see The Mismade Man.* They'd put me in the cabinet of cubes and then let their little ones slide the blades in with their sticky cotton candy fingers. Then they would stack and restack me out of order and laugh and laugh until it felt like someone was sliding a blade into their sides. The cubes with my waist and head in my hands, after the show I'd walk back to campus and put myself back together again without the help of all the king's horses and all the king's men.

Do I sound unfair? It's not the muscly villain with superhuman strength and the biggest guns from cartoons and movies we should fear, my son. It's the neighbor who closes their curtains after they call the police because they saw me walk your sister to school; it's the group that pulls out their phones at the site of an accident to record the carnage instead of to call for an ambulance; it's the guidance counselor who tells you to look into "doing something with your hands" because your skin makes her think gardener, mechanic, construction worker. Think about the Hannah Arendt we've read.

> They knew, of course, that it would have been very comforting indeed to believe that Eichmann was a monster, even though if he had been Israel's case against him would have collapsed or, at the very least, lost all interest. Surely, one can hardly call upon the whole world and gather correspondents from the four corners of the earth in order to display Bluebeard in the dock. The trouble with Eichmann was precisely that so many were like him, and that the many were neither perverted nor sadistic, that they were, and still are, terribly and terrifyingly normal.

I know we've said you should be a person of virtue, that you should help when and where you can, both friend and stranger alike. And yet, as much as I know how right and good our encouraging the goodness of your heart is, what the world will do with your heart fills me with worry because I know what it has done with many others like it. Take good care. Check the locks twice. Love laughter. And keep your smile sharp.

Just now I searched on the internet for my obituary. What does it mean when a person of sound health does such a thing? Is this a monstrous act, a violation of the will to live? Or is such an act related to Freud's argument that a wish for peace is a wish for death, as a friend once put it? If it's the latter, then maybe in searching for my obituary I'm really seeking a nap. I have yawned at least a half dozen times in the last ten minutes.

No, I'm not suicidal, mijo. Please don't worry about that. I would not take my own life. Such a funny phrase, "take my life." No one gets worried if someone says I'm going to take a vacation, take a nap, take out the trash, take a picture, take my time, take down the Christmas tree, take off my shoes, take us to dinner, take up yoga, etc. Shouldn't we want to take our lives into our hands? Is that not the first step to making something of that life? Maybe in religion lies the root of the negative connotation our language gives to "take your life." The Christian Bible teaches submission to the will of God. In that arrangement, our lives are not our own but rather His. Moreover, it is His power and His alone when our lives both begin and end, and thus to take your life is to take your life away from God's control. It's no surprise a nation that is supposed to be founded on Christian principles would yoke the words *take* and *life* together in a negative way.

I'm just sad. Sad about the world you are entering.

And tired. No, exhausted.

Exhausted by the daily assault of cowardice in the leadership of our country. In his letter *De Profundis*, Oscar Wilde writes, "Where there is sorrow there is holy ground. Some day people will realise what that means. They will know nothing of life till they do." When Wilde says "holy," I don't believe he means "religious," though it will mean that to some. What is holy is that which is outside of time. Which is more real: you reading these words of mine or you reading my face as I cradle you in my arms? The moment in which I even conceive of that question marks my stepping foot on holy ground. T. S. Eliot might have had Wilde's sorrow and holy ground in mind when he wrote the opening of *The Four Quartets*.

Time present and time past
Are both perhaps present in time future,
And time future contained in time past.
If all time is eternally present
All time is unredeemable.
What might have been is an abstraction
Remaining a perpetual possibility
Only in a world of speculation.
What might have been and what has been
Point to one end, which is always present.
Footfalls echo in the memory
Down the passage which we did not take
Towards the door we never opened
Into the rose-garden. My words echo
Thus, in your mind.
                    But to what purpose
Disturbing the dust on a bowl of rose-leaves
I do not know.
            Other echoes
Inhabit the garden. Shall we follow?
Quick, said the bird, find them, find them,
Round the corner. Through the first gate,
Into our first world, shall we follow
The deception of the thrush? Into our first world.
There they were, dignified, invisible,
Moving without pressure, over the dead leaves,

In autumn heat, through the vibrant air,
And the bird called, in response to
The unheard music hidden in the shrubbery,
And the unseen eyebeam crossed, for the roses
Had the look of flowers that are looked at.
There they were as our guests, accepted and accepting.
So we moved, and they, in a formal pattern,
Along the empty alley, into the box circle,
To look down into the drained pool.
Dry the pool, dry concrete, brown edged,
And the pool was filled with water out of sunlight,
And the lotos rose, quietly, quietly,
The surface glittered out of heart of light,
And they were behind us, reflected in the pool.
Then a cloud passed, and the pool was empty.
Go, said the bird, for the leaves were full of children,
Hidden excitedly, containing laughter.
Go, go, go, said the bird: human kind
Cannot bear very much reality.
Time past and time future
What might have been and what has been
Point to one end, which is always present.

My plan to only type you an excerpt of this first section of "Burnt Norton" went out the window when the language caught me in its tide. In spite of the anti-Semitic language in some of his earlier poems, Eliot could build a line. He lays out my thoughts on time brick by beautiful brick much better than I ever could. Did you recognize the thrush? You should. I've read you Whitman's "When Lilacs Last in the Dooryard Bloom'd" enough times. In the rose garden of "Burnt Norton," the speaker is given the gift of being in all places at all times. The pool is drained, the pool is full, a cloud passes, and the pool is empty once more. So that you don't think the speaker is lost in some delusion, the thrush urges him to go because "human kind / Cannot bear very much reality."

Sitting in the yellow glow of my office as the early darkness fills my window, I feel I am everywhere and nowhere at once. I am a boy looking up at my mother's face, then looking down at yours, then up again as you hold my hand for the last time. The reality of my life in this moment is that I am also bearing all the hate that has ever been tossed at my grandfather and grandmother and father and mother and brother and you and your sister and your mother and her mother and father and sisters and brother. The next time someone looks at me with a venomous eye, I should tell them, *You cannot bear very much reality*. I am the pool that is both empty and full in their lives. But who is their thrush, who is the bird to guide them, who is the bird that will say *Stay, stay, stay* instead of *Go, go, go*?

What did I find when I searched for my obituary? In 0.25 seconds 210 results appeared. On the first page I discovered Tomas Morin was born in 1682, 1850, 1868, 1872, 1882, 1848, 1873, 1904, 1911, 1935, 1946, 1968, and on and on. I also found the obituary for your abuelo in the *News of San Patricio* that I did not remember having read.

Joe Morin Sr., 70, of Mathis, died Friday, Feb. 23, 2018.

Mr. Morin was born May 15, 1947, in Wheatland, Wyoming, to Jesus and Simona Morin.

He was preceded in death by his parents; a son, Jessie Morin; sisters, Tanislada Sosa, Consuelo Diaz and Guadalupe Padron; and a brother, Ovidio Morin.

Survivors include two daughters, Lisa Garza and Samantha Morin; four sons, Joe Morin Jr., Julian Morin, Tomas Morin and Juan Morin; sisters, Josie Huddleston, Emily Ramirez, Janie Castro and Mary Ortega; 17 grandchildren; and two great-grandchildren.

A rosary was recited at 7 p.m. Monday, Feb. 26, at Dobie Funeral Home.

A mass was celebrated at 10 a.m. Tuesday, Feb. 27, at Sacred Heart Catholic Church. Burial was private.

Survivors . . . we bear the present so that we can survive it. A hermit thrush sang to me one winter when my father was dying. I sought the future tonight and found the pool was both full and empty. And in the leaves, in the leaves we were children laughing.

And what does all this somber digging mean? It's not somber, my son. Did you not hear the laughter only a mere eighteen words ago? I wonder if those other Tomas Morins liked to laugh as much as I do.

Have people learned how to laugh again in your time?

A couple of years ago we all laughed at a reality TV host running for president. We're not laughing anymore. And even when we do, it doesn't have the ring of joy that it used to. Maybe it rings hollow because our current laughter at President Trump is not happening in the present; maybe our laughter today is actually the memory of someone twenty, thirty years down the road looking back at our time. If we can be the memories of the unknown future, then why can't we climb the ladder the other way too? When I googled my obituary last night, I was trying to remember the future. And in that instant, I became 2018 Tomas Morin looking back at 1682 Tomas Morin. How easily those 336 years collapse, how little they mean. I am your future, my son, just as you are my past.

Carlo Rovelli, the theoretical physicist whose work your mother introduced me to, in *The Order of Time* writes, "The notion of 'the present' refers to things that are close to us, not to anything that is far away. Our 'present' does not extend throughout the universe. It is like a bubble around us." While clocks started counting our seconds back in the fourteenth century, it was our country that first became obsessed with making the world follow a standard version of time. This is impossible and a delusion. When I call your mother at 7:00 p.m. from the East Coast, the sun is long gone, and night has slid its feet into the slippers of the forest. But on her end of the phone, the sun is still bright and has not yet set fire to the Texas horizon. My present is not the same as her present, even when technology lets us talk to one another in real time. When I am here in New Jersey and you are there in her belly in Texas, I am from the future, and you are in the past. The son precedes the father counter to our ideas of how time is supposed to move. From within our bubble, it is so easy to forget that the world is full of so many presents. Our perception forms that bubble. But language, language also can make another bubble, one that contains the past, present, and future.

This book is such a bubble. So long as this book exists, it will sit like a stone in the river of time. This doesn't mean it is immortal. Everything is erased sooner or later. But in this book, you and I will still be dancing long after we've turned to dust and are only memories of the people who knew us.

I keep thinking about the stones I found that represent the lives of those other Tomas Morins. Their stones are also made of language: birth and death certificates, marriage licenses, census data. Is one type of language more durable than another? Which has a longer half-life: an epithalamium or a marriage license? Did those Tomas Morins also write letters to their unborn children? Did they spend time away from them, as I am, before those children were born?

It would somehow relieve me of the self-consciousness I feel writing to you in this way. My God, you can't even pick up a pencil at this moment, much less read a word! And yet, I feel like my life—yours, somebody's—depends on my writing to you now. I feel the lash driving me to my desk every day, especially on the days when I resist. And what does it say that sometimes I like the way it feels, that there is a force urging me to hasten these words onto a page that you yourself will probably not read for another decade? What is at work there?

When the fire of creation is hot, I have always worked quickly, feeling the very temperature of my body rise, manifesting the increase in entropy. I don't want to talk about entropy, though. How I've resisted that word about a concept that still feels murky to me. Yes, it's different than energy. Is that not enough? Are you insisting? You are insisting.

You want to hear it in my words instead of in the metallic voice of your robotic tutor. Very well, future boy, here goes: *I am agitated!* Does that suffice? I thought your mother and I taught you to love riddles. When I sit here and write you, this book collides with me and agitates the molecules of my body. That agitation creates heat that passes from me into my chair, desk, and the keys of the computer I now touch. All of these objects will lose that heat and eventually become cold again and at rest. But if I construct these sentences just so and stay true to Robert Frost's "the best words in the best order," then maybe, just maybe, these sentences will hold the heat of my body until the day you pick up this book on your own. On that day, my son, I hope that when these words collide with you that they have enough heat to raise the temperature of your body. When you feel your face flush and your heart quicken, know that this is how I felt the first time I held you in my arms.

"No why. Just here," said John Cage. Okay, but which "here"? It matters immensely. Rovelli tells a story of two friends. One lives in the mountains, the other on the plains. If they set their watches to the same time before returning to their homes, when they meet up again years later, their watches will show different times: "[T]he one who has stayed down has lived less, aged less, the mechanism of his cuckoo clock has oscillated fewer times. He has had less time to do things, his plants have grown less, his thoughts have had less time to unfold. . . . Lower down, there is simply less time than at altitude."

The "here" of John Cage is not universal. Imagine you are the friend who has lived in the mountains. You meet up with your friend from sea level and notice a glow about her. Her skin seems tauter than yours, there is a youthful bounce in her step that you haven't felt in yours for some time. You say to her, *What's your secret? It must be the sea air . . . do you get to the coast often . . . it's your diet, isn't it?* She says she never has the time to get to the coast, that her life is as busy as yours is. What neither of you know is that time has moved by more quickly for you in the mountains. Science can measure this. What's more, they know why it happens. Rovelli tells us the following:

> The Earth is a large mass and slows down time in its vicinity. It does so more in the plains and less in the mountains, because the plains are closer to it. This is why the friend who stays at sea level ages more slowly.
>
> If things fall it is due to this slowing of time. Where time passes uniformly, in interplanetary space, things do not fall. They float, without falling. Here on the surface of our planet, on the other hand, the movement of things inclines naturally toward where time passes more slowly, as when we run down the beach into the sea and the resistance of the water on our legs makes us fall headfirst into the waves. Things fall downward because, down there, time is slowed by the Earth.
>
> Hence, even though we cannot easily observe it, the slowing down of time nevertheless has crucial effects: things fall because of it, and it allows us to keep our feet firmly on the ground. If our feet adhere to the pavement, it is because our whole body inclines naturally to where time runs more slowly—and time passes more slowly for your feet than it does for your head.

When you crawled around on all fours, my son, time passed more equally for your feet and your hands. But now, now you are tall, maybe even taller than me already. All this business about time being relative makes me think about how we spend our days. How much of it is close to the ground where time is slower? Cage doesn't have to worry about a "why" because his "here" is pleasant enough. His line of thinking appeals to a leisure class. Think about what life is like for the people who spend their lives bent over in a field as pickers. Time moves so much slower for them. Where was I going with all of this? My train of thought arrived in the station two days ago, and by the time I finished reading the Rovelli book yesterday, the train pulled out of the station for parts unknown.

Let's see, let me forget the order of whatever point I was going to try to make and just tell you what thoughts I remember. There was something about how you should never move to the mountains, my dear boy! At least not if you want your face to look like an old catcher's mitt. That's an old Seinfeld joke.

Imagine that you lived in a cabin in the woods high up in Colorado, surrounded by lakes and elk and the fresh mountain air of Pikes Peak. And while you're there you eat clean, hike, and don't drink or smoke. But your chain-smoking friend who lives at sea level in Tampa looks fresher and younger than you. Am I saying that you should move to Tampa? No . . . well, you can if you want. Maybe it won't feel odd to you the way it does to me. I've visited it twice, and each time I came away ill at ease. The place felt off. Not the beautiful city and its nice people, but the sky, the trees, and the land. The air felt empty. The light felt old. I felt as if I was walking around in someone's memory of a moment in time that had lost the buzz of life. In a way, a place like Tampa that is almost exactly at sea level—its elevation is forty-eight feet—is both older and younger than other places. Think about how much less time has passed in the Tampa area than in the Rocky Mountains.

Stale! That's the word I was struggling to find. The place felt like a piece of bread that has been left sitting out for too long. Corpus Christi, the city where I was born, feels the same way, and its elevation is even lower at seven feet. One could say that to walk in Tampa is to walk around in, say, the 1800s, whereas to walk around on Pikes Peak is to walk around in 2050. What if elevation sickness is not just our body adapting to the new level of barometric pressure, but also to walking around in a different period of time? If you moved from Tampa to Colorado, then you would in effect be time traveling into the past. That would make anybody lose their lunch.

The head and the feet, that was the other thing I had planned to write to you about because when I read that one's feet are younger than our heads due to our feet being closer to the ground, I thought of slaves and immigrant laborers who spend so much time bent over working the earth. They spend more time closer to the ground than do the people who abuse their labor. As a result, not only are the lives of enslavers and the enslaved marked by differences in money, diet, health, justice, and education, but also time spent near the massive pull of the earth. In the past, we would have thought about those laboring in fields as needing to work fewer hours, and while it's true no one should work twelve-hour days in a field, no one should spend that much time so close to the earth.

Why? I forget. I was excited about the point I was going to make, and then it slipped away. It had something to do with how cruelty is exactly what we expected, manifold and as insidious as those who perpetrate it against others . . . there was going to be some connection to how at least there was some sort of accidental cosmic justice in that enslavers would age faster than the people they treat as nothing more than things . . . and how because they spent so much of their lives farther away from the ground than their slaves in the field that they were unknowingly catapulting their bodies into the future faster and thus toward death . . . but all of that is the optimistic side of me speaking, the side that, if given a moment, will see the other side of the coin and realize that being bent so closely to the ground for so much of one's life also makes those hours of brutal labor longer and feel unending. And they feel longer because they are. Your abuela's father spent most of his life working in the fields while I've spent most of my life upright walking tall, so what was my point? It's gone, mijo; my train of thought is nothing more now than smoke chugging back at me as it heads off to a station where I already sit waiting for you.

When I was a kid and people would ask me, *What do you want to be when you grow up?* I would always say, *A cartoonist.* That was true. I loved the Sunday comic strips. But there was another answer that I kept to myself, an answer that I never shared with anyone, not even my family. That answer was so secret that I forgot about it until this very moment. I wanted to be the train conductor that rode in a caboose. In 1981 Atheneum published *One for the Rose*, one of my favorites of Philip Levine's books. The cover is red, white, and black and is a detail of a map of Detroit. Go pull it from the shelf and take a look. I was five when this book entered the world. Eighteen years would pass before I would find it in the basement of a library in Baltimore, in a city where I felt unwanted, much like in Madison. Inside the book I encountered so many poems that did what Rovelli says getting closer to the earth does; they slowed down time, and in so doing, gave me a chance to find my balance. This is one of those poems.

THE CONDUCTOR OF NOTHING

If you were to stop and ask me
how long I have been as I am,
a man who hates nothing
and rides old trains for the sake
of riding, I could only answer

with that soft moan I've come
to love. It seems a lifetime I've
been silently crossing and recrossing
this huge land of broken rivers
and fouled lakes, and no one has cared
enough even to ask for a ticket
or question this dingy parody
of a uniform. In the stale,
echoing stations I hunch over a paper
or ply the air with my punch
and soon we are away, pulling out
of that part of a city where the backs
of shops and houses spill out
into the sunlight and the kids
sulk on the stoops or run aimlessly
beneath the viaducts. Then we are
loose, running between grassy slopes
and leaving behind the wounded
wooden rolling stock of another era.
Ahead may be Baltimore, Washington,
darkness, the string of empty cars
rattling and jolting over bad track,
and still farther up ahead the dawn
asleep now in some wet wood far
south of anywhere you've ever been,
where it will waken among the ghostly
shapes of oak and poplar, the ground fog
rising from the small abandoned farms
that once could feed a people. Thus
I come back to life each day
miraculously among the dead,
a sort of moving monument
to what a man can never be—

someone who can say "yes" or "no"
kindly and with a real meaning,
and bending to hear you out, place
a hand upon your shoulder, open
my eyes fully to your eyes, lift
your burden down, and point the way.

Freud said, "Everywhere I go, I find a poet has been there before me." Some of what quantum physicists have discovered about time, and how it is relative and collapses, is already contained in this poem, isn't it?

While my memory isn't what it used to be, I do recall seeing one red caboose pass by my house when I was a child. We lived one block away from the tracks. When I would hear the train in the distance I'd go outside and walk toward it. I'd watch the whole thing go by, hoping to see the caboose at the end. How I longed to escape those long, hard days. Later, tucked in bed, I would imagine myself standing on the back of a train as town after town stretched away from me. Always I was in a conductor's uniform and hat, a mustache like the one I wear now, and in my hand, a lantern would swing back and forth in the dark that swallowed me up. When you are lost in the dark, may this letter be a light you can follow. When the world is cruel, listen for your mother's voice; it will come to you softly at first and then louder as it cuts through the night like a train that can carry you home.

WITH LOVE,
YOUR FATHER

I Am What I Yam

It was exhilarating. I no longer had to worry about who
saw me or about what was proper. To hell with all that,
and as sweet as the yam actually was, it became like
nectar with the thought.

—Ralph Ellison

My dearest Jack,

Is that what we'll still call you by the time you arrive next
year? After I finished typing the previous page, I stretched my
arms and legs out. I looked like a starfish in my office chair. It
was still light outside. I texted your mama, and she asked what I
would do to celebrate. I told her I was going to walk into town for
some Indian food. Not even halfway there, I saw a Thai restaurant that reminded me of your mama's favorite Thai restaurant
back in Austin, the one you won't let her eat at right now. Have
you changed your mind about spicy food now that you're in the
world? The joint was empty because it was between lunch and
dinner. They sat me at a table for four by the window. Every time
someone shot me an ugly look from the sidewalk, I pretended
I was Frank Sinatra in a restaurant that had been cleared out
just for him, and that outside there was a line of one hundred
people waiting for me to finish eating. Oh, how I took my time
that day.

So much can happen in another twelve weeks. The world has proven that to me in the last twenty alone. This year I lost my father to cancer, a man I hadn't spoken to in almost two decades. I accepted a job teaching on the East Coast. I fell in love with your mother. Then we found out you would join us. I was forty-two years old when I learned about you, mijo. Even though my back had been acting up for years, I still felt like a pup in many ways.

At first you were just an idea to me. A happy one, to be sure! I think it's this way for many men. While your mother carried you I only had fear grow inside me week by week.

Fear about your health.

Fear about being a good father.

Fear of how this country would see your skin and what they would say your skin said about you.

There was hope too. But it was small. You were an idea I could keep safe inside the pink walls of my brain. This went on for some time until the first time I heard your heartbeat. At that first appointment, we thought they were going to draw some of your mother's blood to see if her blood was also now your blood. But then the nurse prepared the fluid and the wand and then just as suddenly as if I had been hit by a truck, there was your heart. It beat faster than I thought any heart could. You were a humming-bird inside your mother. After we left, she said you felt like a fragile butterfly cupped in her hands in the middle of a fire. The world often feels like it's on fire these days.

The phone in my office is on the fritz. When it rings the quick pulse reminds me of your heart. And when I lift the receiver hoping against hope a human voice waits for me on the other end instead of a fax machine, I am happy that it is the fax machine because just maybe you're missing me too, and you're using a superpower only known to the babies of absent fathers to reach out to me all the way from Texas to say hello.

How I miss you.

I know you can hear voices now because the night before one of my flights back to New Jersey, we were in bed, and I was reading to your mother from Philip Levine's *What Work Is*, and you moved. First I read the funny "M. Degas Teaches Art & Science at Durfee Intermediate School." Next was "Gin" and then "The Sweetness of Bobby Hefka." It was after the last line that your mama said she felt you move. I asked her where, and she placed my hand on her stomach and told me to keep reading.

And there it was. There you were.

You heard me. Heard us.

I don't have my copy of *What Work Is* here in Madison, so I pulled it up on Amazon and tried to scroll through the preview to the Bobby Hefka poem so I could share with you here the words that left my lips when I first felt you move, but I couldn't because the preview didn't include that poem. Instead, the preview ended in the middle of a poem titled "Fire":

FIRE

A fire burns along the eastern rim
of mountains. In the valley we
see it as a celestial prank, for
in the summer haze the mountains
themselves are lost, but as the night
deepens the fire grows more golden
and dense. On this calm ground
the raw raging of burning winds
that cuts the eyes and singes the hair
is seen as a pencil-line of light
moving southward. I know my son
is there, has been for four days,

And the preview just cut the poem off there. The speaker is talking about his son who is a firefighter, but how can I not think of you guarded by your mother in the raw furnace of the world?

What does one call moments like this? Coincidence, fluke, kismet? I like the word *wink*. I mean I like it for its own sake but also to describe a moment like this. Does the word *wink* like me back? Hard to know.

Who can divine the hearts of words? For the first few months of your life, the universe has been winking at your mother and me in just this way. Or not the universe. What have I called it? The totality. Yes, that's it, the totality. What Nietzsche says about the abyss staring back at us if we stare too long into it is wise.

Maybe I am the abyss to the people who stare at me in town. Not because there is anything abysmal about me but because I am so many of their fears suddenly made manifest. It's as if they suddenly face the horror that the brown bodies they fear in their mind really are brown bodies in the moving world.

And what's more, sometimes one of these brown bodies puts on a pair of shoes and walks into a town where white bodies live, and the brown body buys kettle chips, lunch meat, lettuce, tortilla chips, bread, and pickles as if that brown body were now going to live in the town of white bodies, the town where the only brown bodies are the ones that are allowed to visit so they can do what brown bodies are allowed to do in a town of white bodies: cut grass, serve food, pump gas, and other assorted tasks that do not make a brown body a frightening body.

But enough about the monsters of the mind.

Where was I? I remember, your mother will mention something, or I will, and then the phrase "the totality" will pop up again in a wholly unexpected way, the kind of way that makes one smile. If Nietzsche is right and there is an abyss that one can stare into, then its opposite must also exist, what we shall call the Totality. Or Love, surely we could call it that too. If the Totality exists, a conglomeration of all that exists, and if one stares into it, then why wouldn't it also stare back and give us a sly wink to let us know that it sees us too?

I have such mixed feelings being so far away from you. From the campus of Drew University, I am 1,724 miles away. If I drove without stopping, I could reach you in twenty-five hours. A train would take just over two days. But if I flew, I'd be in your mother's arms and talking to you in only three and a half hours. So close and yet so far.

I wonder what my abuelo would think if he were alive to see me traveling away from my family to work in another state with you on the way. Would there be shame in his eyes because of all the grit he used to emancipate his children from the fields of farmers, because his dream for his children and grandchildren never to be apart from their families due to work was now dashed? Well, only his dream for me. All my other relatives have done well.

Forgive my sudden fits of romanticism. They are a nuisance and are often precipitated by a mention of one of those pesky absolutes like *always*. But yes, my abuelo, if I could tell him the stories of settling in here in Madison, New Jersey, I know that he'd laugh. I can hear his smoker's laugh that always ended with a cough. Making him cough was one of the secret pleasures of my childhood.

I can see you sitting on his knee.

His hand is around your waist.

You both stare deep into me as I tell you about my apartment underground. The building is against a hill, so after I walk in the front door, I take one flight of stairs down to my door. Once inside, from one window I have a glorious view of people that starts with their feet as their bodies stretch up to meet the ceiling. The next window over cuts them in half as they walk downstairs. I call that one the head window. If I have the blinds up, sometimes the heads look in, but often they don't. They just keep bobbing to the next window where my eyes are even with their feet.

I have a chair that faces this foot window. I sit here in the evenings and watch the squirrels in the forest and the feet. When someone's eyes catch mine, they look away fast. Unless they were one of my students, I don't think they'd know me from Adam or Fred. Before you ask, no, I don't think they see the abyss when they see me. They startle because I remind them that eyes and heads don't just live up in the air; the ground has eyes too. And those eyes are attached to heads that contain hopes and dreams. Did you know that Madison calls itself a borough? Do you know what rhymes with borough? Burrow! And do you know what lives in burrows? Many things live in burrows, actually. But here on campus groundhogs live in burrows.

Correction: groundhogs and I live in burrows.

The Spanish word for groundhog is *marmota*. It's an ugly, generic word that comes from the French *marmotter*, which means "to mutter." I doubt the person who came up with that word ever had a conversation with a groundhog. But you already know how I feel about groundhogs and names because you must have that Ellen Bryant Voigt poem I read to you every night memorized by now:

GROUNDHOG

not unlike otters which we love frolicking
floating on their backs like truant boys unwrapping lunch
same sleek brown pelt some overtones of gray and rust
though groundhogs have no swimming hole and lunch
is rooted in the ground beneath short legs small feet
like a fat man's odd diminutive loafers not

frolicking but scurrying layers of fat his coat
gleams as though wet shines chestnut sable darker
head and muzzle lower into the grass
a dark triangular face like the hog-nosed skunk another
  delicate
nose and not a snout doesn't it matter what they're called I
  like swine

which are smart and prefer to be clean using their snouts
to push their excrement to the side of the pen
but they have hairy skin not fur his fur
shimmers and ripples he never uproots the mother plant
  his teeth
I think are blunt squared off like a sheep's if cornered does he
cower like sheep or bite like a sow with a litter is he ever

attacked he looks to me inedible he shares his acreage

with moles voles ravenous crows someone
thought up the names his other name is botched Algonquin
but yes he burrows beneath the barn where once a farmer

dried cordwood he scuttles there at speech cough laugh
at lawnmower swollen brook high wind he lifts his head
as Gandhi did small tilt to the side or stands erect
like a prairie dog or a circus dog but dogs don't waddle
  like Mao
with a tiny tail he seems asexual like Gandhi like Jesus
  if Jesus
came back would he be vegetarian also pinko freako homo

in Vermont natives scornful of greyhounds from the city
self-appoint themselves woodchucks unkempt hairy macho
who would shoot on sight an actual fatso shy mild marmot
  radiant
as the hog-nosed skunk in the squirrel trap both cleaner
  than sheep
fur fluffy like a girl's maybe he is a she it matters
what we're called words shape the thought don't say
rodent and ruin everything

Words shape the thought . . . don't ever forget that, my son.

In the twenty years that I've been a teacher, I've always winced when a student calls me professor. Why? Because before today, before this semester, I was what's called a lecturer. That's a teacher with less security. I worked hard to get my degree and then even harder to become the best teacher I could. There were a few years when I taught seven classes a semester between two different schools. The name for that is *freeway professor*. Some would also say *crazy, wacko, not for a million dollars*. What's funny is I did it for far less than a million dollars.

For a stretch, six of those seven classes were freshman composition. On the nights I couldn't stay awake while grading, I'd take my batch of papers to the Alkek Library at Texas State. In the basement floor, I'd find an empty table and get to work. Two or three essays in and my head would nod. When this happened, my pen would stop moving, and I'd leave green ink stains on someone's essay about Marx and the evils of capitalism. That was my cue to pack my bag and move one floor up, where I'd repeat this scene. On every floor I would struggle to grade another couple of papers. By the time I made it to the seventh floor, I'd have graded at least twelve papers. Double digits. I'd grade two more and quit for the night. While packing my bag, I would look out the windows at the flickering beams of light on the interstate in the distance and be filled with envy at the people in the cars who were on their way somewhere fast. When I told the poet Brigit Pegeen Kelly this story, she said I should write an essay about climbing out of the belly of the library in this way. I said I would but never did. She wrote that scorpion poem you love.

Instead of an essay, here I am telling you, our sweet Jack. Do you know what happened at the end of class on the first day of the fall semester? One of my students shook my hand and said her name was Hannah. She then said, "Should I call you Dr. Morín or Mister—" I interrupted and said, "Or you can call me Tomás." She said, "How about Professor?"

Words shape the thought.

Telling students to call me by my first name for so many years had a purpose. It was my way of avoiding that wince if they called me professor, the feeling that I was pretending to be something that I was not. Of course shame was behind my wincing. And why should I have been ashamed when lecturers do much of the same work that professors do?

But now here was the moment when I was finally *Professor Morín.*

I still had to reckon with the fact that while I was now a professor, I was also a migrant professor. For generations, my mother's family did migrant work alongside so many others in the fields. My mother grew up picking cotton. She was lucky because her father never made her do this. She did it because she wanted to be close to him. My father was a hard worker. My mother is still. I like to work. Some fools wouldn't call what I do work. I show students how to be better writers.

Those who think teachers only work when they're in the classroom should see us in our offices at eight in the morning, or now, at eight in the evening, long after everyone has gone home to eat dinner and watch television. I ate dinner too, but then I came back because in writing to you like this, I am writing in a way that I have never written before. Of course I have written letters, but never one so long as this or one upon which so much hung in the balance. The world is a dangerous place, and there are people who have not even been born yet who will be raised to hate you. If Jesus crawled out of his burrow and walked around in this country with his hair of lamb's wool and dark skin many a good upstanding white Christian would call him much more than a *pinko freako homo.*

How can I protect you from these people? I cannot, and yet I hope that in reading about my life underground that you will find some key to your future safety that a part of me has left hidden for you, hidden even from myself. And because that key might just be in my digressions, something your mother and I both love to indulge, I will write to you about what I do and who I am and who I hope to be and every blessed thing in between.

The day I moved into my burrow, I borrowed a red cart from the post office so I could move the boxes with my clothes across campus to where I was staying. The cart was so loud I sounded like a drum line. People stared and I tried not to care.

I wonder if red is your favorite color. I like blue and green. Blue green is even better. But green green is the best.

The morning was cool, and even though the wind moved through the trees, my sweaty shirt told a different story. The sound made me think of how Seamus Heaney's book *The Haw Lantern* opens.

The riverbed, dried-up, half-full of leaves.
Us, listening to a river in the trees.

When I was done moving, I sat in my chair in front of my open windows and closed my eyes so that I could see that river in the trees. As long as my eyes were open, I couldn't fool my ears into thinking they were hearing anything other than the wind moving through the leaves. Try it sometime.

If the trees are tall enough and the wind strong, close your eyes and listen to the white river above you, moving over and around rocks as it foams and speeds on its way to places you've dreamed of where, when the land becomes flat, the water slows, and time stretches long and thin like taffy, because the river is brown and clear now around your knees, and you can't tell where you end and it begins.

This river makes me feel subterranean even when I emerge from my burrow. You can find me in this place surrounded by river sound. You can find me all around you, in fact. At the end of

Chekhov's story "The Black Monk," the black monk tells Kovrin, "I exist in your imagination, and your imagination is part of nature, which means that I, too, exist in nature."

So it is with you.

When you can't find me, think of my voice. When it springs to life in your mind, look around, and you may find me in the rattle of the cicada or my mustache inching across a delicious leaf or my lips in the skin of plums. There is no limit to where you may find me. This applies to your mama and sister and even Boomer too.

The imagination and nature are one and the same. But take care because just like someone you cherish can exist in your imagination and then nature, so, too, can someone you despise. Take me, for example. The idea of me manifest in nature is what the racists who despise me see when I walk into town.

Should this be a cause for fear or hope?

Both.

This fact should make you cautious around those who might hate us. But it should also fill you with hope because the imagination is the battleground; it is the place where hearts can be turned for good or ill. Be wild with your imagination but also careful with it. While working in his bean fields in the country, from time to time Thoreau hears far away, now near, the sounds of military music. He writes:

> When there were several bands of musicians, it sounded as if all the village was a vast bellows and all the buildings expanded and collapsed alternately with a din. But sometimes it was a really noble and inspiring strain that reached these woods, and the trumpet that sings of fame, and I felt as if I could spit a Mexican with a good relish—for why should we always stand for trifles?—and looked round for a woodchuck or a skunk to exercise my chivalry upon.

Scholars have suggested that in this moment Thoreau paints himself like a New England Don Quixote. He was on the record as being against the Mexican-American War. Some say that he's pointing out how the narrowness of patriotism can plant in the imagination the seeds of violence and hatred. For example, the noble military music makes him feel as if he could drive a stake through a Mexican, roast him over an open fire, and then eat him with relish. Because there are no Mexicans around, he looks for a woodchuck or skunk to skewer instead.

Do you see what I meant about how the imagination can be dangerous if someone is careless with it? Be better than Thoreau and use your imagination for good. Don't use it to create loss in the world. Be a maker, not a destroyer like the people who see me on their sidewalks and in their stores and think, *I could smash me some beaners with ham today.*

I used to feel ugly. Have I told you that?

In years past I would have thought how ugly they must see me, the barbarian in their garden. But not now. Though I have come to the knowledge of my own beauty late in life, I have come by it honestly, and while my beauty alone would be enough to gall them, that I know that I am beautiful makes their gall more bitter, so bitter that not even a gallon of relish would be enough to wash the taste from their mouths.

Every angel is terrifying. Rilke wrote that. My hermano C. Dale Young reminded me of it just now when he saw a photo of me with silver wings against a soft sky tossed blue. Maybe when I walk down the street in Madison, I am the dark angel of their worst natures. New Jersey is the Garden State. Maybe some of them think it's heaven, or as close to heaven as they can get. Or maybe they think New Jersey is their own little Eden on earth, and I remind them of the angel standing at the gate of Eden, bored out of his mind, twirling his flaming sword.

They forgot I existed, but now they remember. And they see that I've upgraded my sword to a machete. I carry it in my mouth, and its flames will strike them dumber.

Maybe this is why their children are so afraid of me. The scales on their eyes are still thin, so they can see the fire that would deliver them from their ignorance . . . forgive me, when the wind bends the trees like it is doing right now, my nature tends to topple to the biblical.

I'm on a fruit farm in Michigan with my friend Emilia Phillips. We're reading our poems tonight in Kalamazoo. I'm staring at the giant trees and listening to the first river in the trees I ever met. That's right, I said met. One has to meet a river before one can say they know it. In both a ground river and a sky river, it's so easy for me to become invisible. I love to disappear into the everything that is around me. Traveling reminds me how different we all are and lucky that it is so. This semester that I've been away from you, I've traveled to the following places to read my poems:

39°57'11.592" N, 75°11'31.4808" W
40°40'41.4372" N, 73°56'38.976" W
40°43'28.5888" N, 73°59'47.3892" W
30°15'53.927" N, 97°44'47.76" W
42°17'30.1416" N, 85°35'14.0172" W
41°5'26.3472" N, 73°55'4.494" W
36°40'7.68" N, 88°18'59.796" W
40°43'35.724" N, 73°59'23.352" W

Can you find them on a map? While their names are different, they are all the same distance from you and your mama: away.

Did you know that when two groundhogs fall in love, they share a den until the mama is pregnant? Then the father leaves and doesn't come back until the babies arrive. Your mama and I are accidental Marmota sapiens. I can't wait to return to our burrow in Austin so I can help hold you and rock you and bathe you and teach you about the ways of our kind. How to take care of the dens in our burrow, how to walk and chew and laugh like no one's listening.

We'll show you how to guard against prowling predators like the hawk and owl, the fox and dog, and most dangerous of all, the human. Many burrows are near roads, so you have to be careful when walking. Last week on my way to work, I was nearly run down by a human. I saw him coming, so I moved to the edge of the road, and as he came up behind me, he was close enough that if I had reached out when he passed by, my arm would have been inside his car.

Coincidence? Owning a brown body will make you question what you think you know about coincidence. So watch out on roads because many of our kind have been run over or shot on roads by humans who hate us. Humans will also make up stories about how our burrows make their neighborhoods dangerous. It's not enough that we live underground and out of sight; some days I think the only burrow where we could be safe from them is a grave.

When I looked out the window at the farm's apple trees, I noticed a fly in the window. I thought it was a baby fly, though maybe it was an adult and Michigan flies are just smaller than Texas flies. It buzzed nervously against the glass, so I spoke to it in the way I always speak to Texas flies. In a soft voice, I said, "It's okay. I can help you if you let me, brother. Here, jump on my finger and I'll carry you outside."

"Bzzz bzzz . . ." it said before hopping off.

"Okay, then jump in my palm and I'll close you up with my other hand, but I promise I'll let you out when we get to the door. Okay?"

"Bzzz bzzz. Bzzz bzzz . . ."

"That makes you nervous, huh? I don't blame you. I wouldn't want to be locked up in some giant hands either. Okay, then, how about this? I'll gently pick you up by the wing and take you outside? Will that work?

"Bzz bzzzzz . . ."

I picked Brother Fly up by the wing, just like I used to with the Texas flies that would get trapped in my apartment, and released it out the front door to go do what flies do. Whenever people hear these stories, they think they are flukes, magic, unbelievable. It makes me sad that a simple kindness is seen as fluke, magic, unbelievable. But that's the world we live in, mijo.

Cruelty is cheap. You can find it on any sidewalk day or night. But kindness . . . kindness has become a rare thing. If you cross paths with someone who believes kindness is fluke, magic, unbelievable, do not be surprised if they swat at you with the rolled-up newspaper of their disgust. If they even read. And if they don't, well, worst of all are the cretins who would try to smash you with their bare hands.

Humans in the United States have become quite an unpleasant subspecies indeed. They are nothing like one of your namesakes. Yes, we gave you the name Francis because we love the nickname Paco and also because it is an old family name on your mama's side. But Francis is also the name of my favorite saint. Remember the story of Saint Francis and the wolf? When people retell that story, they often say that Francis tamed the wolf with his holiness. Or they say that God tamed the wolf as a favor to his beloved Francis. None of this is true at all. That version of the story only serves to support Genesis 1:26, "And God said, Let us make man in our image, after our likeness: and let them have dominion over the fish of the sea, and over the fowl of the air, and over the cattle, and over all the earth, and over every creeping thing that creepeth upon the earth."

Propaganda!

Propaganda of the worst kind!

This line of dangerous thinking has been used to rubber stamp abuse and cruelty against our animal brothers and sisters. I can hear my old vegan comrades rattling their sabers because I have returned to the tribe. Alas, it is not so. I'll tell you more about that later because if I don't make this point now, then I will surely forget it. My memory isn't what it used to be, you know. Where was I?

Oh yes, the story of the wolf.

While cleaning out the attic of an old library in Italy, workers discovered a trunk of medieval manuscripts, one of which contained the story of the wolf. While the original Latin author is unknown, scholars believe the translator was Susanna di Galles, a nun who was renowned for her vast erudition. What follows is my translation of her Tuscan dialect of Italian, the very one which Dante used to compose his *Commedia*.

There once was a poor family in the forests of Umbria who went hunting for mushrooms and berries. With every step they took, their feet crunched the old brown leaves of autumn. The mother, father, daughter, and son checked along every tree and under every bush. They were so hungry that they forgot they had picked the forest clean the previous week. The days when they would roast rabbit and deer now seemed like a dream that had happened to some other family. It had been weeks since they had heard a bird sing or a rabbit hop across the forest floor. Nobody knew where the animals went or if they would ever come back. In the nearby town, no one was hungry because they had all the sheep and chickens they could eat.

One day, the father and mother couldn't get out of bed. The daughter saw that hunger had sent her parents into a deep sleep. Her brother said he was cold and crawled under their parents' bed. He tucked his pale face against his knees. She stroked his hair and thought, *My brother has turned into a snail*. She left him there and went into the forest to look for food. She decided she wouldn't come back until she had found something for her family to eat.

The little girl walked and walked until she passed the green pond she was supposed to stay away from. She wondered if she could eat anything that might live in the pond. Could she eat a frog or a lizard if she found one? She walked the valley a long time until she found a thin trail that went up. By the time she had climbed the hill, she was so tired she sat against a tree on a patch of soft moss. Her eyes were heavy. They hung lower and lower. When she felt something wet against her hand, she had been dreaming of catching a frog in the pond. When she looked at her hand, she saw a dead rabbit. Its fur was wet and warm. She looked around and saw a brown wolf watching her. The wolf had blood on its lips, but this did not scare the little girl because she knew the blood was the rabbit's.

The little girl stood up and said, "Thank you, Brother Wolf. This rabbit will save my mother, father, and brother. I thought all the wolves in this forest had been hunted and killed. Where did you come from?"

The wolf said, "There are many things humans have forgotten or do not know. I am not your Brother Wolf, I am your Sister Wolf. Feed your family, then return here alone tomorrow when the sun is at its highest, and I will tell you my story."

When the little girl returned home, she lit the fire and began to clean the rabbit. When the smell of the boiling rabbit filled the house, the little girl's mother and father and brother awakened. They rose slowly and stared at the little girl pouring soup into four bowls. The father said, "Where did you find this rabbit, Chloe?"

"In the forest, Father," said the little girl.

The mother said, "How did you ever catch it?"

"I didn't. A wolf gave it to me, Mother."

The eyes of the brother grew big as acorns.

"The wolf said if I returned tomorrow when the sun is at its highest to the spot where I saw her that she would tell me where she found the rabbit."

The father shook his head and said, "Absolutely not. It's too dangerous!"

The mother said, "But what if the wolf tells her where all the animals have gone? This soup won't last forever."

The father knew she was right and that they had to take the chance.

That night, with full bellies everyone slept for what seemed like weeks. The next morning, the father walked his daughter to the door and drew from his pocket a small knife with a handle made from an apple tree. He gave it to his daughter and said, "This knife is small, but it might help you if the wolf lunges at you. Keep it close, Chloe. And never forget that we love you."

The daughter hugged her little brother, mother, and father and then walked into the forest. She walked past the pond, through the valley, and up the hill. At the mossy tree where she had rested, she found the wolf.

"I have returned, Sister Wolf. Thank you for the rabbit that saved my family's life. Please tell me your story," said the little girl. The wolf nodded and proceeded to tell her story.

"When I was a just a pup," said the wolf, "my grandfather would tell me about a man he once met in this forest. The man's name was Francis. He was not like other men who loved to hunt and kill wolves. My grandfather knew this because he did not smell death on the hands of Francis. He had smelled the hands of Francis from far away. When he saw Francis walking into these very woods one day, my grandfather asked Francis why he was not afraid of the woods where men had died."

Francis said, "Because I know that you are my brother, and my brother would never harm me."

My grandfather said, "You are not like the men from the town who have forgotten that we are all brothers and sisters. How is it that you have not forgotten when everyone else has?"

Francis sat down, crossed his legs, and said, "Because when I was a baby, a fly would land on my pillow and whisper to me all the secrets of the world that people had forgotten. She had no children to tell these secrets to, so she chose to share them with me."

My grandfather walked over to Francis, licked the wounds on his hands, and said, "Who cut your hands like this?"

"My god in heaven marked my hands and feet in the same way that the hands and feet of his son were marked," said Francis.

"Who marked the hands and feet of the son?" asked my grandfather.

"Angry men who had forgotten the secrets of the world," said Francis.

"What is it you would like to ask me, Brother Francis?" asked my grandfather.

"Why did you kill the animals and men from the village?" asked Francis.

"I killed the animals because I was hungry. I killed the men because they wanted to hurt me for being hungry," said my grandfather.

"Why did you eat the animals of the village instead of the animals from the forest?" asked Francis.

"Because the men of the village killed and drove off all the animals that used to live in this forest. What else could I do to keep from starving?" said my grandfather.

"I would have done the same thing, Brother Wolf," said Francis.

"Tell the villagers that if they feed me and allow the animals of the forest to return, then I will spare their lives and the lives of their animals," said my grandfather.

Francis considered this idea and then said, "So it shall be." From that time on, my grandfather and our family never went hungry. Even when time passed and people once again killed and drove off the animals that had returned to the forest, we had enough food to eat because while the animals of the forest seemed to have vanished to people, we always knew where we were. I gave you the rabbit yesterday because you were hungry. If you and your family promise never to forget that we are all brothers and sisters, then you will not go hungry again.

Chloe hugged the wolf around the neck and thanked her. She told the wolf that her family would promise. The wolf watched her walk down the hill and through the valley, heard her pass the pond and walk into her house. Through the sound of the lonely wind in the trees, the wolf sat still and listened to the little girl far off in the distance telling the story to her family. The wolf heard the little girl's family shout as they poured four bowls of soup. She had heard the sound of human joy many times in the distance and knew it well. She knew that time would tell whether the forest had just now grown kind or cruel.

Do you see now, son, why I honor the life of a fly? No? In time you will.

Remember that one afternoon I told you to ask Boomer to explain to you what gentleness is? Close your eyes and see him roll onto his back to show you his pink belly. Do you see his four tiny brown nipples and hairs softer than cotton? And do you remember how we took your hand and showed you how to gently rub that belly given to you so freely in trust? Did you see then the light pink skin jagged like a bolt of lightning where his testicles had once been? When I think of your little hand in that moment learning both love and kindness, I remember Nietzsche saying, "O my soul, I gave you all, and I have emptied all my hands to you; and now—now you say to me, smiling and full of melancholy, 'Which of us has to be thankful? Should not the giver be thankful that the receiver received? Is not giving a need? Is not receiving a mercy?'"

A few times I tried to be merciful and kind when people stared at me in town. I asked myself, *What if through their eyes they're not seeing me as a ghost just risen from a cemetery? What if they see something else?* In those moments when my anger and fear subsided, those moments when some unknown well of patience was tapped, and hope rushed through me like water from an underground spring surging toward the surface, my thoughts grew "more golden and dense." I asked myself, "What if they see me as someone they admire? Someone they could follow? Someone come to lead them out of the dark of their lives? And if this is so, then would it not be an insult, a crushing blow if we are to be honest, to those same fragile spirits that yearn with such earnestness for my gaze? Don't some of them look at me with the same mix of awe and envy that is on the crowd of faces anytime the English Queen or her grandsons go about in public? What if in the darkest, most unexcavated parts of their hearts, they really want to be ruled by someone who looks just like me?"

People like to say that anger can drive someone mad, and while this is true, so can hope. On those days when hope soaked the fire in my brain, I would fill the pools of my eyes with the benevolence of a royal. In order to play the role, I would need a backstory, so I would tell myself that I was a prince who was wearing the crown of crowns for the first time because the king they had known for decades was now cold in the ground.

It always made me laugh to think of my father as a king. And so as the son of a king who was now king himself, I was walking into town to mingle with my subjects for the first time, to let them read the charity on my face and know that their futures were secure because I would not take so much from them that they would be left in a state of want. Ever "more golden and dense" my thoughts until I was in it, and I would nod to a select few of my subjects. I reasoned that if I nodded to all of them, then they might suspect I was not the new royal who had come to rule over them. Nobility does not so casually dispense acknowledgment. In fact, to find an example of a person who nods at everyone they cross paths with, one would need to look no further than those who serve nobility themselves.

It would be disastrous if they thought I was a cook or a valet. If they even suspected such a thing, then I'm sure someone would have hastily led me into a kitchen and fitted me with an apron upon which my name had already been monogrammed. Or worse yet, they might hand me their bags of groceries and lead me to their car.

To complete the picture, I would add a slight smile to my occasional nods and the glance of aristocratic mercy with which in those brief moments I graced their common lives. I was surprised how many of them seemed all too ready to be ruled, ready for a steady hand to give their plain, uneventful lives meaning because after all, is not one of the unspoken purposes of royalty that it gives humanity something to strive for that can never be reached? Tales of commoners marrying into the aristocracy are the exceptions that prove the rule. Kings and queens and emperors and empresses have long claimed to be related to whatever divine beings their people worshipped. A royal is a god on earth.

When the steam from the fire in my brain was thickest and my thoughts were their most "dense and golden," I would think, *I am your god*.

I am your benevolent god.

Once, when I was in the grip of these thoughts, I saw a man in a coat with a fur collar. He was a stout man with shiny shoes, exactly the kind of man one would suspect was a town leader. As this banker or doctor walked toward me, I hadn't made up my mind which he was. I imagined him being so overcome with the magnitude of my presence that he would take off his coat and offer it as a gift. He would show me the silk lining, the buttons made of maple. Then he would ask me to feel the fluffy collar that was made from groundhogs. Sick to my stomach at the thought of a groundhog being killed for its pelt, I would rip the collar off and throw the coat on the ground, and as I raised my arm to strike this man, he would fall to his knees and say, "It's you! A prophecy foretold of your coming centuries ago, a king whose fist would be wrapped in the fur of a groundhog. All hail the Groundhog King! All hail the Groundhog King!"

When I thought of that I was enraged, my son. I would lower my gaze for the rest of my time in town and finish my errands as quickly as possible so that I could return to the safety of my sub-sub-basement back on campus. I wish in a moment like that when my spirit had been ravaged by an excess of hope that the veil between this world and the next would have lifted so my father, Jackie, was no longer invisible, and having seen the state of my tortured soul, he would offer me one of the two yams he was carrying home. I would have peeled back the foil of my yam one leaf at a time before taking my teeth to its soft, warm skin.

We would have clinked yams as if they were wine glasses and laughed. And when the ache in my stomach was gone and all that was left were our peels, we could have gone up and down the street smashing the skins of our yams against the faces of a relish lover who would gladly spit on a Mexican. And each time we worked one of those sweet peels like a sloppy kiss against the face of one of those foul creatures, Jackie would chant, *The power of Yam compels thee*, while in my most tender voice, right next to their ears, I would whisper, *I am what I Yam. I am what I Yam.*

I saw a white-tailed deer on campus this morning. I've seen deer in and around towns all my life, but when I saw this one, the trees all around us like matches with their heads afire in orange and red and the sidewalks vanished under the wet lick of gold leaves, this deer trotted away from me as if he—it was a he—was out of a dream, a dream deer, and as such perfect in the way all dream deer are perfect, being made as they are out of the memories of every deer one has seen.

Time ceased to matter as he went gliding away.

He was beyond sound.

Beyond time even.

As he moved away he took with him the bubble of his presence, and with every step he took, he moved me closer to the edge of his life and thus to the moment when we would no longer live in the same time.

Severing from him caused a great sadness to well up within me, and when we were lost to each other, I turned the corner and saw a red fox. It stood at the entrance of a groundhog burrow.

Was it a he or a she? you ask.

I guessed a male by the shape of his head, but I can't be sure. What I do know is that before he ran off, he smelled worry on my body, and I saw hunger and cold crouch in his. I took a loud bite of my red apple to bare my big teeth and their allegiance to Brother Groundhog. I know he will be back. Maybe not today, but in a few weeks when the students are eating turkey with their families and the ground is as white as this page.

In the mid-1800s, Americans on the East Coast bored with hunting gray foxes let red foxes from Europe loose in the forests. Because gray foxes have claws like a cat, when they're chased by dogs and hunters on horseback, they often climb high into trees. Did you know this? Humans believe if death is quick, then it can't be a sport. The hunger of foxes has brought death to ducks and birds and groundhogs. A group of foxes is known as a skulk. A group of groundhogs is called a repetition. A group of humans is called a crowd. On December 17, 1845, crowds of humans read John L. O'Sullivan's words in the *New York Morning News*: "And that claim is by the right of our manifest destiny to overspread and to possess the whole of the continent which Providence has given us for the development of the great experiment of liberty and federated self-government entrusted to us."

Crowd is both a noun and a verb.

Words shape the thought.

Crowds of humans devour land and life. Skulks of foxes eat berries, birds, grasshoppers, squirrels. Repetitions of groundhogs eat clover, buttercup, berries, insects, and the best vegetables in a garden.

Poppy seed . . . sesame seed . . . lentil . . . blueberry . . . kidney bean . . . grape . . . kumquat . . . fig . . . lime . . . pea pod . . . lemon . . . apple . . . avocado . . . turnip . . . bell pepper . . . heirloom tomato . . . banana . . . carrot . . . spaghetti squash . . . mango . . . ear of corn . . . rutabaga . . . scallion . . . cauliflower . . . eggplant . . . butternut squash . . . cabbage . . . coconut . . . jicama . . . pineapple . . . cantaloupe . . . honeydew . . . romaine lettuce . . . swiss chard . . . leek . . . mini watermelon . . . small pumpkin.

For weeks we were told you were the size of all of these foods. A groundhog would probably eat all of these, but it would never eat you. It's so strange and funny to think of you as a cabbage right now. Your abuela calls cabbage "repollo" in Spanish. *Repollo* has its roots in the Latin *repullulare*, which means "to sprout." Maybe a group of humans should be called a cabbage instead of a crowd. A cabbage of Europeans spread murder across the North American continent, believing their God gave them permission to do so. When they felt most lost, they bowed their heads and prayed, "Our Cabbage who art in cabbage, Cabbage be thy name. Thy cabbage come, Thy cabbage be done on earth, as it is in cabbage. Give us this day our daily cabbage. And forgive us our cabbage, as we forgive those who cabbage against us. And lead us not into cabbage, but deliver us from cabbage: For thine is the cabbage, and the cabbage, and the cabbage, forever."

There were years when I tried to eat like a groundhog. I didn't want any blood to be spilled for my stomach. Then one day my body turned against the butterfly in my throat. I even hung on for a while after I found out the pills that were supposed to help me were made ineffective by soy. And then to hunger I gave in. Now I take new pills that are even made from pigs.

When a pig is being slaughtered, someone cuts out their thyroid so it can be dried and pressed into a tiny round pill. Have you seen a pig in person yet? I hope so. If not, then we are bad parents and must remedy this immediately. Among their other names—woodchuck, moonack, red monk, thickwood badger—a groundhog is also called a whistle-pig. Even though they don't travel in a whirlwind like Chekhov's black monk, I've always liked "red monk" the best as a name because there is something holy about them; in their burrows they remind me of the prophets living quiet lives of contemplation in their caves. "Groundhog" is not even a good name. It's like calling a crow an airbird or a trout a waterfish.

A red monk can move over six hundred pounds of soil to dig her burrow. Each burrow will contain multiple rooms; there will be sleeping quarters, a pantry, a nursery, and even a bathroom. Every burrow has a handful of entries and exits. The tunnel systems of many burrows can measure over forty feet. The red monks that live here have almost doubled in size since I arrived in August. They will hibernate soon. While the world above ground is frozen, underground they have lowered their body temperature to thirty-five degrees, and their heart can beat as slow as five beats per minute. My father's heart was down to five beats per minute the last time I saw him alive.

If you look at pictures of me from five years before I sat down to write you these letters, you might think that I've been preparing to hibernate too. I haven't doubled in size, but I did put on thirty pounds in one year, the year my body forgot that the butterfly in my throat belonged to it. If I had been planning to sleep for twelve months straight, then the thirty pounds would have been fine, but no such luck. Everything is working now, and you probably don't even recognize me in photos from 2018, although my voice is the same voice that you hear from inside your mama's belly.

Your abuela and your abuela's mama also had bodies that forgot they carried a butterfly inside. I hope yours doesn't, and if it does, we will help you find a doctor that believes you. Tell them the story of our bodies if they don't. It took me years to find a doctor who would believe the story of my body's betrayal. My story helped your abuela find a doctor who would believe her. Her mother was not so lucky. Sometimes doctors believe we don't feel pain, that our bodies are less sensitive than white bodies. As my sister Vievee once said, when they treat us this way a doctor stops being a doctor and becomes a veterinarian. When we visit them for help, they don't see a human, they see a dog or a cow walk into their office.

Did you dress up for Halloween? you ask.

Am I rambling again? I know you don't like it when I talk about how unfair the world is in this country. I can't imagine that I will ever write anything that will matter more to me than these letters. I have poured so much of my hope for your future into them. This moment is so heavy with possibility. Even now as I type, there are cells in your body that are mixing pigment for your skin. Every door is still open to you because no one can see you yet, my little invisible man, and yet I can sense some of those heavy doors dragging shut because they know what we can't know.

As for your question, you already know the answer. No, I didn't dress up. Why put on a costume when a lot of the people in town believe I already look like a perfectly scary monster as it is? Have I told you what the Vitamin D3 pills I've just started taking are made of? The fat of sheep's wool. Can you believe that? A slick, woolly pig is just a groundhog by another name, if you ask me.

The first frost is on the ground.
The world is whiter than usual.
More empty too.

Is that my echo? I hear.

And with that the song begins that I've by now listened to hundreds of times in the last few weeks. I sit in my sub-sub-basement with my headphones on and stare out the window with Prince's "17 days" on repeat. The last gold of light and leaf disappears as night falls.

Is that my echo?

When the sun is tucked away like this, I like to hunt for what I know I can't see. Deep in the dark of the forest there is a tree limb gilded in fungus. It's as big around as my body and twenty feet in the air. Day and night it pulses as if it never knew what it meant for the sun to set.

Give me the straighter one, says Prince, and then he hammers a rhythm on the piano that rearranges my blood. I imagine his engineer watching, his hands poised over the board as if it was a piano and they were playing a duet. It is 1983 and I am seven years old. This recording will be thirty-five years old when you hear it for the first time, and yet the beat could have been recorded tomorrow or yesterday or all the time in between those two ideas that can't contain how this song has captured an endless present.

Can you turn the lights down some in here?

I rise, turn off my lamp, and walk to the window. I kneel on the couch under the window and stretch my hand to the glass. It feels warmer than it should. I think I can see a flash of yellow in the treetops, but I can't be sure because the window is dirty, and the hazy reflection of my face is a gauze on the forest. I open the window and crawl onto the ground as the melody pulses in my heart.

Good God.

I try to stand but can't. When I try there is a weight on my shoulders that won't be lifted. I smell soil all around me. I sink my fingers in the dirt and go on all fours for what seems like days. I look and look for the shine in the trees with no luck. I move toward a soft crackle in the distance. As I go I call out, *Hello! Hello!*

The crackle stops and then I hear, *Turn the voice down a little.*

"Who is that? Who's there?" I ask.

"I am. Who are you?"

"Who are you?" I ask.

"Is that my echo?"

"Hey, I'm no echo. Can't you see me?"

"Come a little closer," the voice says. I crawl toward the emptiness ahead of me where the air seems less dense. Then the ground under my hand is not there, and I tumble head over heels into a hole. When I finally stop, I roll onto a bed of dried leaves. A red monk is studying a leaf in his tiny hands that shine like black leather gloves. We are in a room shaped like an egg. The floor is packed with leaves, feathers, and pinecones.

"What is this place?"

He walks over to a patch of floor and sets down the leaf carefully. Then he turns it left, then right, and finally flips it and turns it once more. He squints at me and says, "My bedroom."

"You sleep here?" I think about what it would be like to sleep here for months in something like a coma and exist somewhere beyond the world of clocks.

"Of course I do. Where do you sleep?"

"In a bed."

"Is it underground?"

"Yeah, sort of."

"Well then you're not as dumb as you look."

"Hey, what's with the attitude?"

I am still on all fours, and my back hurts. The red monk waddles over to me. He is like a burlap sack with legs. As he comes closer I see his claws and two long teeth and fear what he might do to me with them even though I taste nothing like the clover they are said to love. He places his hand on the small of my back and gently pushes down. "Fold your legs," he says. As I do, he places his other hand on my chest and says, "Now straighten up." The feeling of relief wraps my body like a blanket.

"I live here. I can have any attitude I want," he says.

"I'm sorry. I'm lost and not used to crawling around like this. And my back hurts all the time."

"I know."

"How can you know?"

"Because I've watched you walk around up above. I see how uneven your step is. And I see how your shoulder drops. I'm guessing your feet hurt too."

He has not moved his hands the whole time he has spoken to me. Each one feels like the comal in my grandmother's kitchen. His easy kindness unwinds me, and I begin to weep. He holds me in that way until all of my tears are spent.

"Oh, baby now. You might be ready," he says.

"For what?"

"To return to the surface. Follow me."

My back loose, I drop back on my hands and follow him to a tunnel that leads up. The more we climb, the less my body hurts. My shoulders are no longer uneven because stooped over as I was underground, they didn't hang. The cool soil between my toes is soothing to the blisters that have brought me so much pain. Weeks seem to pass as we climb, and then the ground levels off, and he stops at the entrance to a room.

"Where are we?" I ask.

"Go inside and look. There's someone waiting for you. I'll wait for you here."

The air from the room smells like mulberries that were picked and left in the sun for too long. I hesitate to go in because I don't know how anyone could even know that I would be here. I step in and find a man smoothing a wall of earth with a trowel. He wears jeans and boots but no shirt. His back is to me, and with every swipe of his trowel, I can see his muscles swell and relax like snakes. His skin looks purple in the dark.

"Hello," I say.

"Que pasó, mijo?"

Sound moves slower underground, so before his words reach my ears, I know it is my father. I hear him before I hear him.

"Dad, what are you doing here?"

"Staying busy. Just cause you die don't mean you're dead. You're only dead when you stop workin'. That's when you're dead dead."

I am stunned to find your abuelo here. In the world of clocks, it has been 285 days since he passed, 410,400 minutes since I kissed his forehead and said goodbye. And now here he is in a burrow.

"Do you live here?"

"Sometimes when old Red wants company. Which ain't often." He laughs.

"What is this room? Why are you here?"

"Red calls this the pantry. There's acorns and shit right on the other side of this wall. I made the wall to keep the food from burning when it gets cold upstairs." He sweeps the trowel left to right in long, smooth strokes and packs the soil in.

Why are you here?

I hear the words, but I don't know if they've come out of my mouth or his. I watch him work and wait to see if he will say anything. When he doesn't, I finally say, "I'm looking for the light." I have no idea why I say that because it makes no sense to me nor would it likely make any sense to him.

"Well, shit, you're in the wrong place then."

His laughter annoys me. "I didn't mean light like a light; I meant light like goodness." I can't believe I said that. Who even talks that way?

"You're still in the wrong place for that, boy. Ain't no good or bad down here, just sleep. Just food and sleep. You need to get back up top where you belong."

"I don't belong up there. People are mean to me and—"

"Is that all? Shit, I thought I raised you better than that, boy."

I don't like the way *boy* comes out of his mouth, so I say, "Maybe the problem is you didn't raise me."

Left to right, left to right, beads of soil roll to his knees with every pass. He's like a metronome.

"I thought with all the disappointment I put you and your mama through, you wouldn't be surprised anymore when things didn't go your way. Don't you know life ain't about being happy? It's about not being dead."

"I don't believe that. When you weren't there someone else taught me about hope. And about happiness."

"Well, it's on them then."

"What's on them?" I ask.

"How you feel . . . you being disappointed and crying cause the world is mean to you. I thought the only *sin was in your skin.* But caring is a sin too. You can't give a shit, mijo."

"I don't believe you. My skin isn't a sin. If it is, then you're to blame, you son of a . . . you can go to hell."

"I already did. No work there, so I left."

My head begins to spin, and if I were not on my knees, I would surely fall. I feel a warmth on my shoulder, and when I turn, I see the red monk's tiny hand steady me. "It's time to leave," he says, and so we do.

I follow the red monk up another tunnel. From behind, his big haunches look like a bass fiddle. He's humming a song that I know. Every so often his steady hum breaks into a few percussive *do-do-doo-doos.* The soil between my fingers and toes feels cool. I think about how I spoke to my father. I had never in life taken that tone with him. Silence and anger were the weapons of my disappointment.

Why couldn't I just notice the racism less? And when I did notice it, just not care, as he said I should? That would make life so much easier. No, I couldn't do that, I wouldn't turn myself into a callus. Before the callus the skin blisters and fills with anger. Then comes the pop, the drying and hardening, and then the blister again until the skin your parents gave you is misshapen and old. I wouldn't make a shield out of not giving a shit. Doing so would be the same as admitting that my feelings don't matter, that I don't matter. I would not let anyone deny my humanity.

The tunnel levels out again, and we stop. The red monk says, "I can go no farther because the season is late, and I need to sleep. Those two tunnels both lead to the surface. Choose whichever one you want."

"I, I don't know what to say . . . thank you."

"I hope you find your golden tree," he says and then wobbles toward the tunnel. I hear a loud whistle as the air hits his teeth, and he slides down the tunnel like a subway car.

On that landing, I debate which is the best tunnel to climb. When I stick my nose in one, the air has the faint scent of wood cleaner and soap. And along the wall of the tunnel, the roots of a tree vibrate gently with the sound of music. I place my dirty palm against the root, close my eyes, and listen. A cymbal and drums. *This tunnel must open up in the grass outside the chapel*, I think. I walked by once and looked up to see the open window of that sacred wooden room from which there poured a solo the drummer kept stopping and restarting. During my time underground, my sense of smell and my hearing has gotten stronger. My eyesight too.

I crawl over to the other tunnel and sniff. Dust. Glue. The library! *I know exactly where this leads*, I think. The exit is on the side of a hill facing the setting sun. A group of small trees behind the hole provides a windbreak. My sub-sub-basement is not even three hundred feet from here. If it's still dark, I can crawl out and make my way back before anyone sees me and asks why I'm covered in dirt. I make my choice, and as I climb up this tunnel, I think of excuses I could give for my appearance should I happen to cross paths with anyone. *I was playing rugby*, I could say. The field is muddy after all. But what if they ask who I was playing with? I've never played rugby, but surely no one plays it by themselves like other sports. I climb and climb until I encounter a wall of dirt.

Have I taken a wrong turn? I wonder. Has the red monk played some sort of trick on me? Surely not. He has only been kind to me. I could have asked for no better Virgil. And yet, where is he now when I need him? Could he have filled in the exit before his hibernation and simply forgotten? If so, I will dig my way out and then pack it back in for him so that no hungry fox can dig in and pounce on him while he sleeps.

Is this what it must feel like to be buried alive? I wonder. At least I'm not in a box. Life is all around me in the form of drowsy millipedes and snails and roots of all shapes and sizes. This is the opposite of death. As my arms grow heavy, I hear a foot tapping a beat faintly. The sound grows louder as I fill and empty my arms with soil.

Then I hear, *Come on down baby now . . . fancy new day . . . yah uh . . .* and I am at my window, shivering. The temperature must have dropped twenty degrees since I opened it.

I shut the window and put on my sweater. The sky beyond the forest is growing a pale pink. The sun will be up soon. Too soon, so I close all the blinds. I'm not ready yet to let the sun into my burrow.

I think about everything my father said, the kindness of the red monk who found me in his home and treated me like family. I turn on two of the burners on my stove and hold my hands over the blue flames. There is still so much left I need to tell you, mijo. Have I told you enough? What more can I say? Now that you are older, do you remember all the days when I was away and not there to help your mother tuck you in at night in your crib? It broke my heart every time I left.

What else can I say?

The land of this country, like so many other lands on this planet, was taken by force. Blood was spilled on it, and that is something the earth does not forget. It is sick in a way that only a true earth dweller can understand; your mama's grandfather was a miner— ask her to tell you about him. In my short time underground, I have felt the full weight of this pain buried in the earth, and I can tell you it is immense. You, too, my sweet boy, were born of pain, but it was a pain made from love. Never forget that.

I have yearned for the sea all my life; its waves were crashing outside my parents' window day and night while I rolled in my crib. The edge of a lake is serene, there's no doubt about that. But the sea is a place of beginnings.

It is the beginning.

When people try to render you visible or invisible by asking where you are from, remember that the world is magical, but it is not magic. Your life is not a white rabbit pulled out of a black hat by white hands in white gloves for applause. Never forget that the top of the hat opens, that the table it sits on has a door, and that under the table there is a cage just small enough for one body to forget what living is. If you do not know it yet, you come from resilient stock: bricklayers, cotton pickers, house cleaners, miners, cooks, truckers . . . you were made to endure. But there is a difference between enduring and martyrdom. Don't be a martyr. Did you know rabbits live in burrows too? When you feel yourself forgetting the difference between a burrow and a cage, find a map and make your way toward palms and sand. My grandmother, your abuela's mother, told me what I am now going to tell you.

Find a beach and sit. Focus on everything that has been vexing you. When you have it fixed firmly in your mind, walk into the water and dunk yourself under the waves. Feel the salt sting your eyes, nose, and lips. Return to the beach and rest. Do this limpia twice more. After you walk out the third time, don't look back at the water. All of the evil eyes and envious tongues the sea has washed away are floating there, waiting for you to look so that they can return to you from the burning water.

When you are done, slip on your socks and shoes.

Don't forget to brush off your feet.

Buckle your seatbelt.

Key in the ignition.

Back up carefully and avoid the sea in your mirrors.

Now drive until you can no longer see the water. Drive away and remember to follow the one commandment Dostoevsky left us with, the one you have heard me say more times than you can ever count: *Thou shalt love life more than the meaning of life.*

WITH LOVE, AS EVER,

YOUR DAD

A Wall Is Indeed a Wall

There, in its loathsome, stinking underground, our
offended, beaten-down, and derided mouse at once
immerses itself in cold, venomous, and, above all,
everlasting spite.

—Dostoevsky

My dearest Jack,

The driver's name was Lenin. Have you heard of that other Lenin
from across the sea? I'm sure you've heard your Marxist mother
talk with vigor about her dear Marx and hegemony and thus her
other beloved, Gramsci, he whose first name is your middle name
in honor of his suffering in prison because of the power of an idea.
Even when Mussolini made Gramsci disappear behind the walls
of a prison, he could not render his mind invisible. But the mind
is the body too!

No, not too, but *is*.

The mind is the body.

We are all body.

Oh yes, what about the driver! Well, he didn't look like Lenin.
Or like a Communist. He looked like he could've been one of your
abuela's cousins from San Antonio or Laredo. He picked me up
before the sun had risen and drove me to the airport. When I
arrived and learned my flight had been canceled and rebooked for
an ungodly arrival time, I asked a young man how long it would

take to travel to the next terminal. Even though I asked him in English, he spoke to me in Spanish. Of course I understood him perfectly. I said "gracias," and while I searched for a new flight on my phone, I saw him wander back to his coworkers who were sorting luggage and say to them, "Man, how about those Astros! They're looking good this year."

I had no words!

Did he think I only spoke Spanish or that Spanish was my more dominant language? Or was he tired of speaking only English at work and jumped at every opportunity to speak Spanish? Twenty minutes later he checked on me to see if I had called the customer support line or needed any other help. He was kind and looked like he could've been one of my nephews from Arlington or Michigan.

That kindness would be a balm after I traveled all day and finally landed in Vermont that night. Earlier in the day I called the driver who was to pick me up and asked if they did pickups at night, especially after ten. He replied by singing in a raspy voice, "All night long, all night, all night long." He was no Lionel Richie, let me tell you, and if I hadn't been spun three ways to Sunday by all the travel cancellations that day, I might have laughed. I could hear the disappointment in his voice when I didn't. He said he'd be there at 10:00 p.m. and took my flight number, and I thanked him.

All buckled up, we pulled away from the airport. His hair was long, and so was his beard. He was dressed in black and looked like one of the Oak Ridge Boys. The one that looks like a wizard. In other words, the kind of person you would want on your side in a fight. We hadn't gone a mile before he asked, "Where are you from?" I mentioned that we had moved to Houston from Austin. With a mixture of joy and regret, he said he had lived in Austin for a few years.

"I lived in Central Texas for over twenty years, and it's changed a lot," I said.

"It sure has. I don't like how the liberals are taking over Austin. They have lots of biracial people there now," he said.

"Hmm," I said as the Burlington city limits stretched behind us and we climbed into the darkness.

"They have all these extra rights that normal people don't have. Same thing is happening in Vermont. When I retire I'm probably moving to the Blue Ridge Mountains."

A cover of Kate Bush's "Running Up That Hill" came on his radio. No vocals or any instruments except a piano. I'd never heard this version before. It haunted the stale air of the taxi. I Shazamed the song, but no dice. Someone else came up. I welcomed the silence while I tried to find the pianist on my phone. You already know it was Paul Hankinson because I've played this song for you so many times.

The driver said, "My son used to work in human services. Went to college and everything."

"That's great," I said.

"He had to leave his job, though. Too many liberals in that line of work too. Homosexuals, girls married to girls. I don't have anything against them. I have a friend who is gay. But a social worker should be straight because some people don't wanna deal with that sort of thing when they go into the office to ask for help."

"Oh," I said as we slid between the Green Mountains on our way to Montpelier, and I wondered what this man thought when he saw me walk out of the airport and get into his taxi. What did he think when he saw my name? Who did he assume I was when he heard my voice?

"You hear this guy playing the guitar?"

"Yeah," I said.

"He's crap. He's only playing in one key. That's boring."

"Hmm," I said.

"You have to switch it up. When I play guitar, I'll play in three different keys in one song. I can sound like three different guitar players."

"Wow, that's impressive," I said.

As "All I Wanna Do" started playing, he said, "I love that Sheryl Crow. She really keeps her looks going. Proud lady. I fell in love with her when we were eighteen."

"You know Sheryl Crow?" I said.

"No, we're just the same age. Problem was I was married and already had two kids, so I was stuck. She still turns me on."

We took the exit to Montpelier and before long were crossing the Winooski River and climbing the steep road up to campus where I would spend the week teaching writers how to use language thoughtfully in order to make poems people might pick up one day and find the mirror for their feelings that they've been waiting for.

Oh, my son, the calculus I did in my head when he said what he said was both quick and long. And you know how math has always befuddled me as much as it delights you. Now don't tell me geometry is math, and how can I love one and dislike the other?

Show my work? Is that what you want; you want to see the calculations I did to arrive at my response to him saying that people who look like you and me ruined Austin? Okay, here is how I landed at my solution of "Hmm."

Scratch Paper 1: Shame

"I don't like how the liberals are taking over Austin. They have lots of biracial people there now," he says.

"Bless your heart."

"What does that mean?" he says.

"You know what it means."

"Are you calling me a dummy?" he says.

"You just called yourself that with what you said."

"Oh, I get it. You must be one of those snowflakes," he says.

"Mister, I have a biracial son. How would you like it if you got in a taxi and the driver started in on how people like your son were ruining everything?"

"Look, buddy, I didn't know about your son. I didn't mean any offense," he says.

"Maybe next time you'll think twice about what you say when you're driving someone."

His face turns red, and his hands grip the steering wheel more tightly. We drive down the dark highway without speaking. "Running Up That Hill" fills the silence, and by the time Sheryl Crow comes on, all I want to do is be out of this taxi, to stop shaking from the adrenaline that is pumping through my body, to stop looking at my GPS to make sure he is still taking me to Montpelier and not somewhere else where no one will be around to watch us sort this all out like "men."

Scratch Paper 2: Anger

"I don't like how the liberals are taking over Austin. They have lots of biracial people there now," he says.

"What the hell do you have against biracial people?"

"They're messing everything up with their whining," he says.

"My son is biracial, you ignorant asshole."

"Who're you calling an asshole?" he says.

"Did I stutter?"

"I don't have to take that kind of abuse," he says.

"Abuse? I call you out for all the dumb shit you just said, and now you're the one whose feelings are hurt?"

"Hey, man, I didn't mean anything by it," he says.

"What do I care what you meant or didn't mean? Would it have been easier for you if I had just sat here quietly and let you run your mouth and not said anything? Huh? Would that have made you feel better?"

"Look, buddy, I'm sorry," he says.

"I'm not your buddy. And you can keep your sorries. The college paid you to drive this taxi, not to say ignorant, stupid shit to the people you pick up. So drive. I don't wanna waste my time talking to you anymore."

His knuckles are white, and he doesn't say anything anymore. "Running Up That Hill" comes on, and he drives faster. Someone calls him, and he can't remember how to cancel the call so just pushes buttons until it stops ringing. Sheryl Crow comes on as we cross the Winooski River, and I wonder how close I came to him leaving me on the road.

Scratch Paper 3: Hate

"I don't like how the liberals are taking over Austin. They have lots of biracial people there now," he says.

"What makes you think things were any better when people like you were running the show?"

"Excuse me?" he says.

"You heard me. All you ignorant white people think the same. You all think you're hot shit and better than everyone else. Well, I've got news for you. Your life is just as pathetic as the next person's."

"You don't know anything about my life," he says.

"Oh, I think I know enough just by looking at you."

"Hey!" he says.

"Did I hurt your feelings, Gandalf?"

"You can't talk to me like that," he says.

"I'll talk to you any way I want as long as I'm in this car. You're a pathetic loser who thinks the world owes you something. What's worse, you think people who don't look like you stole your future. You probably think you were supposed to be a famous musician or something. Well, you can't just look like zz Top and expect it to happen, man. And I got news for you: if it hasn't happened yet, it's not going to ever happen. Ever. Do you understand?"

The car slows down as he pulls onto the shoulder of the highway.

"Lemme guess, you're gonna ask me to get out of your taxi now because your feelings are hurt?"

He walks to the back of the car and opens the trunk. He grabs my suitcase and says, "Get out. Now." I open my door and step out. He sets my suitcase at my feet and stares at me.

"You leave me here and I'll have your job in the next five minutes. I'll tell your boss that either they fire you or I'm gonna sue them until their head spins. I can see the news headlines in the Vermont papers now: Taxi Driver Leaves Professor Stranded. What do you think they're gonna choose: your job or millions of dollars? I bet you wanna hit me, don't you? Do it. I'd love to send your ass to jail."

He gets back in the taxi without saying a word. The only sound is the hum of his engine, the passing cars, and a beautiful rendition of "Running Up That Hill" on piano as he drives away and I stand under the beautiful Vermont sky dotted with stars.

Scratch Paper 4: Rage

"I don't like how the liberals are taking over Austin. They have lots of biracial people there now," he says.

"You fuckin' woodchuck," I say and lunge at him. My hands grab his throat, and the car swerves from one lane to another as he reaches back with his right arm and tries to hit me in the face.

But I hold on and say, "Take it back, take it back." He drives off the shoulder, and the car flies into the air.

Everything moves slowly now. My seatbelt yanks me back, and as we roll the sky becomes like the blackest, most still lake, and the grass is the side of a mountain that is so high you can't see anything beyond or around it. Life is upside down and then it isn't and then it is again.

When I wake up, Sheryl Crow is singing, *All I wanna do is have a little fun before I die*. I can't feel my legs or my arms. My head is wet. The windshield is gone and so is the driver. I think how great it is that Vermont doesn't allow billboards on their highways because I could be lying here staring up at a sign that says, DO BILLBOARDS WORK? IT JUST DID.

I worry that if no one finds me here in the dark, then soon I will be gone too, and there will be one less person in the world to snarl at whatever and whomever means you harm, my son.

Scratch Paper 5: Pity

"I don't like how the liberals are taking over Austin. They have lots of biracial people there now," he says.

"How do you know I'm not biracial?"

"You don't look it," he says.

"And what does biracial look like?"

"Ummm," he says.

"Maybe the better question is, who isn't biracial?"

"I have family that came over on the Mayflower," he says.

"Oh yeah? Well, what about your other family? How many people do you think are one hundred percent pure anything? I did that DNA test, and I'm Spanish, Indigenous, Italian, Jewish, North African, Senegambian and Guinean, and Nigerian."

"That's crazy," he says.

"Hell, it even said that around 1700 I had one relative who was Korean."

"100 percent Korean?" He chuckles.

"Haha, okay, you got me there. But you get my point. When we turn people into labels, then they become less than human. And if history teaches us anything, it's that this only leads to a lot of pain for everyone. My son is probably someone you would call biracial."

"I'm sorry, man," he says.

"Thank you for saying that. You can't just go off saying crazy stuff like Trump because you might have someone in your back seat who's on the edge and just waiting for an excuse to beat someone's ass."

"You're right," he says.

"Last thing you wanna do is to end up plastered on the side of a mountain hoping the car you flipped doesn't catch fire and explode."

He nods his head, and as a haunting cover of "Running Up That Hill" comes on the radio, he changes the station. Bob Dylan sings, *You're invisible now, how does it feel, how does it feel?*

"Bob Dylan sounds the same on every song. Don't get me wrong; I love Dylan. But the key to real good music is variety," he says.

"Amen."

We listen to music silently the rest of the way as the minutes and the miles zip by on our way to sleepy Montpelier.

Scratch Paper 6: Humor

"I don't like how the liberals are taking over Austin. They have lots of biracial people there now," he says.

"That's a weird thing to say. Aren't you biracial?"

"Me?!" he says.

"You look like you're at least 50 percent Vermonter, 50 percent Deadhead, and I don't know about the other 50 percent."

When he laughs the long hairs of his beard shake like a silver curtain. "Mister, you're funny," he says.

"It's been a helluva long day. I thought maybe you could use the laugh as much as I could."

He laughs and says, "The Grateful Dead had some good tunes, but I could never really get into them the way some people did."

"I hear you. I've never really gotten into their music either. Their fans are like a cult, and I'm wary of any group that wants you to belong to them that much."

"I know that's right," he says.

Even though I can't make out Camel's Hump in the darkness, the Green Mountains are just as beautiful at night as they are in the day. "Running Up That Hill" comes on, and I say, "This Kate Bush song never gets old. They could do a version on a recorder, and it would still have the same power to slow everything down while also pumping you up. Like right in the middle of your chest. This song makes you wanna find someone you love and give them a long hug."

"Amen, brother," he says.

Scratch Paper 7: Love

"I don't like how the liberals are taking over Austin. They have lots of biracial people there now," he says.

"That's not a nice thing to say."

"How so?" he says.

"It's not nice to talk about people like that. It's disrespectful."

"I didn't mean no offense by it. I was just trying to make conversation," he says.

"I know, but talk like that hurts people's feelings. And there's enough shit in the world we all deal with every day without us making it worse for each other, ya know?"

"I'm sorry," he says.

"How would you feel if I got in your cab and started in on how these redneck woodchucks were ruining Vermont? And how they were too stupid to see that someone like Trump, their messiah, hates them. Hell, if you were stranded on the side of the road with your thumb out, you'd be lucky if he didn't run you over when he passed you by."

"Hmm," he says.

"He hates anyone who isn't like him. We're not millionaires who can scratch his back, so that means you and me."

"Maybe . . ." he says.

The silence between us fills with "Running Up That Hill," and the soft notes of the piano remind me of sighing in the rain.

"If you were stranded on the side of the road at night, who do you think would stop to give you a ride, me or him?"

"Probably you," he says.

"Heck yeah, I would."

I can't see his smile, but I feel it. And suddenly even the stars feel like they're smiling. I lean my head against the window and think about the beautiful days ahead filled with work and joy in a place I love. We exit, and Sheryl Crow lifts the night when she sings, *I got a feeling I'm not the only one.*

And there's my work, son. I did it all in a fraction of a second. And you already know the solution I chose was fear. And as I committed what the driver said to memory, I pretended that I was a double agent. Someone he would spill all his secrets to. Someone he would reveal himself to as the white supremacist that I imagined he was. I was afraid to choose a path that would lead to a place where I wouldn't be able to see you anymore. Like prison or six feet under the ground. I chose to stay alive for you even as I was dying inside. All I wanted was to get back to you, to our morning drives to your school, to your sweet little voice saying, "I want to hear the clown Plim Plim, Daddy."

Did I ever tell you Bozo was my favorite clown growing up? Or how I would practice pitching ping pong balls into buckets so that I could be ready if the time ever came that a little brown boy from Texas would get to go on his show in Chicago?

I never made it to the Bozo show. I had a chance to move to Chicago and attend DePaul when I was eighteen, but the city seemed too big. Too far. Too much the opposite of the small life filled with big dreams in the tiny town I had grown up in.

Turns out many cities beyond Chicago had their own Bozo Show. Detroit, Boston, Grand Rapids, Bangor, Dayton, El Paso, Miami, and on and on. Bozos were even making children laugh in Mexico, Brazil, and Canada! There was a whole army of Bozos that I never knew about out there all pretending to be the same Bozo.

Bob Bell of WGN-TV was my Bozo, though. He was Bozo for twenty years and was inducted into the Clown Hall of Fame. From what I can tell, neither Bob Bell nor any other person who played Bozo was ever a victim of a violent crime while in costume.

In 2016 reports from all over the globe surfaced of individuals dressing up as clowns to scare, and sometimes attack, the unsuspecting. The situation grew so dire, real clowns started losing work. The clown president even became involved and tried to reassure everyone that real clowns live only to bring joy into the lives of others.

I could only find one mention of a clown arrest. Maybe it wouldn't be so safe to drive around dressed as a clown. When the horns of someone's fear are nearby, perhaps it's best not to be mistaken for a rodeo clown. I would never take you to a rodeo. Or a bullfight.

But I would gladly drive you anywhere else you wanted to go while you sit strapped in the back, singing in Spanish about a clown with blue hair, a red nose, and a white mouth, who says,

If you feel like clapping, then clap.
If you feel like whistling, then whistle.
If you feel like shouting, then shout.
If you feel like laughing, then laugh.

ALL MY LOVE,
YOUR WILLING CHAUFFEUR

The Loves We Share

> From Pandora's box, where all the ills of humanity
> swarmed, the Greeks drew out hope after all the oth-
> ers, as the most dreadful of all. I know no more stirring
> symbol; for, contrary to the general belief, hope equals
> resignation. And to live is not to resign oneself.
>
> —Albert Camus, "Summer in Algiers"

Mijo,

I was eating a red plum when its juices ran all over my hand. It was then that I reached for a bath towel and found the washcloth that I thought had been missing. That whole week that I had been in Vermont, I used only my big hands to scrub my body in the shower. I know you're probably giggling right now and thinking, *cochino!* Nah, not cochino at all. Okay, maybe just a little. But I must confess that it felt good to have no washcloth or loofah between my hands and my own skin. I don't love myself enough. I never have, really. But I'm trying.

The Kafka workout Elena Passarello and I are doing right now calls for "rubbings." A third of the exercises are stretching and rubbing your skin. For example, if you lift your knee to your chest while you're standing, as you lower it, you're supposed to run your hands along your shin, over your kneecap, and then up your thigh to your hip.

J. P. Muller, the inventor of this workout, said that the goal of the rubbings is so that "the entire body gets thoroughly and systematically polished. The rubbing is done with the palms of the hands, and should be a simple stroking or friction to begin with; later on, as one's strength increases, it should be so vigorous that it becomes a sort of massage, if not for the internal muscles further from the surface at any rate for the thousands of small muscles connected with the vessels of the skin."

Why do I mention this? I don't know. Oh! I remember now! Loving ourselves, yes, I have the thread again. From when I was the age you are now, I gave myself to loving my father more than loving myself. I hardly knew what love was, to be honest. But I did know care and what it meant to care for someone with a gentle hand and a soft voice. And this I did for my father, the abuelo you never met because he passed before you were born. He had the illness of addiction, and I feared he would die if I loved myself more than I loved him. I was wrong of course, but what did I know having already spent so much time in "love's austere and lonely offices" Robert Hayden tells us about? I thought a son was supposed to serve his parents and family. I never questioned what a son was or from where that word came. Not like you, hijo de mi vida, mi corazón, who joyfully questions what everything is and what everything is called in Spanish and English. And Korean!

Even so, you already have a better eye than I did, or do, for the odd detail, and what's more, you don't hesitate to call it out. Just yesterday you saw for the first time the Nepalese tiger rug your mama was gifted laid out in the bathroom. I knew you would like the powder blue of the background, but I wondered what you would think about the tiger. When you saw it, you clutched your arms and held them close to your chest and said, "Daddy, daddy, what animal is that?! It's kinda weird."

And it is weird. Indeed, enough to startle you, you who have seen so many animals from around the world already and not to mention have heard their voices and seen them jump and swim and fly on the TV. But this tiger is no tiger at all. It is someone's idea of a tiger, quite possibly a person who has never seen a tiger before in their lives. It is gray and white like the snow leopard, but it has not the leopard's long and elegant ballerina body. No, this tiger has the torso of a wolf, the legs of a bear, and a tail like a snake. The head is even odder than that motley assemblage of body parts. It is ridged like the bottom of a hiking boot. The nose is prehensile, and the face is flat like a catfish.

Labels are the worst of us and the best of us. They are stories we make up about ourselves and the world we are a part of. We are fools to hope that any part of a creature or thing's essence can be contained by a label. And as you know, I have always placed us in the category of creatures too. No doubt we have already talked about all of the vile and racist labels humans have invented for anyone who doesn't look like them, so I won't waste any space here talking about those. No, I want to talk to you about some of the labels that appear innocent, that would fly under the radar because we use them so often that they have all but lost any spark they once contained, and without that spark, we would cease to notice what work they do right under our very noses. Let's turn to our beloved *Oxford English Dictionary*.

> **Male:** (noun) a male person; a boy or man. Chiefly in expressed or implied antithesis with *female*, but also (esp. in *Medicine*) simply as a synonym for *man*. Borrowed from 12th century French. Of human beings . . . of animals . . . of the reproductive organs . . . of plants . . . of minerals . . . of hard and compact sand or gravel . . . of tree bark . . . of an instrument, mechanical device, or connector
>
> COMPOUNDS:
> male aunt
> male bawd

male ingenue
male mother
male virgin
male climacteric
male greensickness
male widowhood
male midwife
male model
male nurse
male prostitute
male stripper
male supremacist
male supremacy
male-determining
male-spirited
male bonding
male—female
male fern
male fool-stones
male gauge
male incense
male menopause
male orchis
male pattern baldness
male pill
male pimpernel
male rhyme
male screw
male sterile
male sterility
male thread
male-dominated

male-bashing
male condom
male impersonator
male-oriented
male rape
male-like

I don't see you or me in any of these words, mijo. The word *male* now looks so strange to me that I honestly don't even know what it means anymore or how it relates to me and my life. And yet, when we fill out countless forms throughout our lives, the worst ones will ask us to identify ourselves as either male or female. The best ones will ask which best describes us: male, female, nonbinary, transgender, intersex, type an answer, prefer not to say. Some forms will even give the option of going by Mx. instead of Mr. or Ms. or any of the other assorted titles. Maybe if the word *male* in the dictionary looked like this, I'd know better what to call myself.

> **Male:** of humans . . . of animals . . . of plants . . . of love . . . of tenderness . . . of joy . . . of patience . . . of light . . . of softness . . . of air . . . of grief . . . of beauty . . . of tears . . . of laughter . . . of you

> **Mexicano/Latinx/Hispanic/Chicano:** a native or inhabitant of Mexico; a person of Mexican descent, esp. a Mexican-American. A person of Latin American origin or descent. Pertaining to Spain or its people; esp. pertaining to ancient Spain. A person of Mexican origin or descent living in the United States (particularly in those areas annexed from Mexico in 1848); esp. one who is proud of his or her Mexican heritage and concerned with improving the position of Mexicans in the United States. Borrowed from Spanish and Latin.

All these words erase the tribes of people who live in what we call Mexico and the southwestern United States today. For all its splendors, language is so poor. The English language has become like masa that's rolled out too wide, so when it leaves the comal, it is not a tortilla but something less. You can eat it and it will sustain you, but the feeling of it between your teeth will be diminished. And because of its brittleness, you won't be able to fold or wrap it around carnitas or anything else. We'd do better with something like this:

Mexicano/Latinx/Hispanic/Chicano: of desert . . . of oceans . . . of mountains . . . of song . . . of gritos . . . of tortillas . . . of Nahuatl . . . of agave . . . of español . . . of pyramids . . . of jungle . . . of dance . . . of tecolotes . . . of rivers . . . of tlacuaches . . . of conchas . . . of javalinas . . . of fry bread . . . of Gila monsters . . . of lake . . . of canyons . . . of nopal . . . of beaches . . . of margaritas . . . of alebrijes . . . of family . . . of siestas . . . of Xolo dogs . . . of mesas . . . of marranitos . . . of us

Mixed/Biracial: not of one kind, not pure or simple; composite; mingled or blended together; assorted; combining different racial or ethnic elements; partly borrowed from French; containing different backgrounds; made up of good and bad, or positive and negative elements; befuddled; an area of land designated for different purposes

COMPOUNDS:
    mixed-ability
    mixed-crew
    mixed-income
    mixed-traffic
    mixed-voice
    mixed bed

mixed border
mixed cadence
mixed-cell
mixed chalice
mixed contract
mixed doubles
mixed drink
mixed earth
mixed economy
mixed fraction
mixed greens
mixed herbs
mixed martial arts
mixed message
mixed money
mixed nerve
mixed nuts
mixed ratio
mixed signals
mixed spice
mixed tone
mixed train

Not only do these words fail to capture anything of who we are, mijo, but they also tell me just about nothing about anything.

The word *racial* comes from the 1800s.

That makes the word not just a lie, but an old lie.

I won't tell you again all the details of how words have been used to keep people shaking with fear of other people because they are one shade lighter or darker. We've gone over all this many times, and I've seen you nod and nod, saying you understand. I believe you because even though you are only three feet tall so far, you already understand so much.

What I want to tell you instead is that purity doesn't exist. Not in people or anything else for that matter. The purest diamond is still only a rock. Enough blood has been spilled to fill a canyon that could be called the Gulf of Diamonds just because fools told themselves that diamonds were more valuable than other rocks.

Because we all agree on this lie it feels like the truth.

We want it to be true.

"Poor people are lazy."

If we say it enough times, then it feels true. If enough people say it with us, then it becomes a truth that we claim is self-evident, like water is wet. Fire is hot. Grass is green.

But is grass green?

Science tells us that we live in a world without color. Your hammerhead shark isn't blue. Nor is a banana yellow. Nor is your soft copper hair the same color as your mama's. They say everything is light, and our brains take in the light it sees and give it color. They even say there is no black or white. How many millions of lives would have been saved if we could unsee color?

Probably not many because we are nothing if not a resourceful species. History has proven this many times over. We would've come up with a different way to measure our differences if put to the test.

But what about the octopus?

What about the cat?

What about our cousin the baboon?

Remember the brain teaser, "If a tree falls in the forest and no one is around, does it make a sound?" The answer is, of course it does because human ears are not the be-all and end-all of receivers of sound. Not only would the sound of the tree crashing to the forest floor be heard by ants, a beaver, a moose with a calf, a mushroom, and countless other creatures, but it would also be heard by the falling tree and its family of trees surrounding it. All science has said is that color is an illusion for us and only us. For all we know, to a bear the grass is purple, salmon is yellow, and water is red. And what color are all these things to the salmon? Who knows?

But what does all this talk of yellow salmon swimming in red waters have to do with you? Everything, my son.

Your favorite thing to say right now when I don't know the answer to one of your questions is, "Let's look it up!" I love your thirst for knowing. Never forget that instead of looking something up, we can always make it up too, just as I made up for us this aquatic family tree that is just as interesting, if not more, than the one compiled from birth certificates and marriage records that our family treasures.

I SING THE BODY AQUATIC

When I offer my sweaty hand in greeting
I can see the future. No matter
how gently you squeeze, I know
when our hands meet you will crowd
my crooked index and pinky fingers
against their straight-as-an-arrow brothers
so that my hand looks more like a fin
than an appendage perfectly evolved
for tying shoelaces or wiping a tear
from the red face of the missionary
who rode his bicycle under the sun
all day to reach my porch.
When he takes my hand he won't find hope
or brotherhood or whatever
he's looking for. Because I can see
the future at times like this
and because I have an unshakeable faith
in the law of averages, I know
when our hands embrace he'll find
proof of natural selection

in the shape of my fingers, evolutionary
holdovers from an era of gills
when the earth was all aquarium
and some distant relative with sleepy eyes
and splayed fins who tired of being mocked
by handsome carp said, *To hell with it*
and climbed out of the sea and across
moonlit dunes toward a sandy life.
In that moment he couldn't have predicted
300 million years later one of his
descendants having long since grown legs
would be belly down on a beach
before an ocean that would carry him
and his own to the land of Montezuma
to roast in the sun for four centuries
where their conversion into dry Catholics
would be so perfect you would never guess
I can't swim to save my life
or anyone else's or that the sound of a wave
pounding a rock makes me nostalgic.
You would never know any of this
until we met on the street
or you knocked on my door and embraced
my hand and felt Galilee on my palm,
which you might mistake for nervousness
unless you were familiar with the embarrassment
of having the only wet fins at a party
because somewhere in your family there was a pike
or two hailing from one of the lost schools
that under pain of death swam
far from the Atlantic or Mediterranean,
around both of which I hear shame
and fear are still the coins of the realm.

I was going to plumb the OED some more for you and dismantle the words *father*, *son*, *gender*, and *health*, but I'm weary today.

American weary
Bone weary
Cat weary
Diamond weary
English weary
Funnel cake weary
Gracious weary
Have mercy weary
Ice pick weary
Jive weary
Kettledrum weary
Lisp weary
Melt weary
Nail weary
Obey weary
Punch weary
Quicksand weary
Rag weary
Salt lick weary
Time weary
Upset weary
Violin weary
Weary weary
X-ray weary
Yearn weary
Zoo weary

I want nothing more right now than to be away from this screen and curled up on this rainy day with your small back against my stomach, hand in hand, our sighs in perfect time with one another as the colorless day slouches in whatever direction it wants because we don't care for anything but the dream in which we share an egg. Who needs a whole egg, after all? I eat the yolk, and you eat the rest until there is nothing left but two smiles, a circle that will be unbroken, forever and ever, amen.

And at some point, we awaken.
Your eyes curl like a smile.
My eyes curl.
You blink slowly.
I blink slowly.
When we speak like this in the secret language of cats, it is all I ever need to know or say on the subject of love.

There is a land where they share my distrust of language, so much so that they've dispensed with the names for violence. They don't use the words *boxing, murder, combat, wrestling, duel, shanking, clash, cruelty, rumble, assault, rage, battle* . . . instead, this land, a place that our beloved Henri Michaux traveled to in his imagination, turned to good old, clean numbers to keep track of the worst of our human impulses. Come, come visit with me. You'll be safe as long as you stay by my side and don't speak.

IN THE LAND OF THE HACS

As I entered the village, I was drawn by a strange sound towards a square packed with people, in the center of which, on a platform, two almost naked men strapped with heavy wooden shoes, were fighting to the death.

Though this was by no means the first time I had witnessed a savage spectacle, the dull, subterranean clop of the shoes knocking against their bodies made me feel sick.

The crowd did not talk, did not shout, it oohed and aahed. A clatter of complex passions, their inhuman moans were lifted and hung like immense curtains around this "shitty" fight where a man would die without any glory.

And what always happens happened: a hard and stupid shoe struck a head. The noble features, even the least of them are noble, the noble features of that face were trampled like a worthless beet. The chatty tongue tumbles, while the brain can't cook up a single thought, and the heart, that little hammer, takes its turn and is pounded, and what a pounding!

Well, he's dead now! To the other one goes the purse and the relief.

"Well," a bystander asked, "what did you think of that?"

"How about you?" I said, for one must be careful in these countries.

"Well!" he replied, "it's a spectacle, a spectacle among many. According to tradition, it's called Number 24."

And with these words, he politely said goodbye.

I was advised to visit Van Province. There is a fight there from which all the others originate. It bears the number 3 among the spectacles, and the men battle in a marsh.

This fight is usually between family members so that the struggle will be greater. It's not hard to guess which pairings are the most popular. The age difference between one generation and another doesn't matter, so long as their physical abilities are equal.

At these spectacles, there's barely a whisper. The slimy mud is the sole host of the combat, impartial but treacherous, at times it exaggerates a simple blow to sound like thunder, and other times it almost completely hides a deadly blow to the stomach, creeping, low, it is always open to the person who has given up. These buffaloes with glistening human limbs, their heads dripping with mud, pant, struggle, half-choked, blinded, deafened by the treacherous mud which enters everywhere and sticks and jams.

I saw a fight between two brothers. For four years they avoided each other, building their strength and getting in perfect shape. When they reunited, they almost didn't realize it. They began to feel themselves dreaming, as they covered with mud all the features that said they were family, features they were about to dishonor so much!

The old hate from when they were children re-entered them little by little, all while they slathered the slimy, leprous soil on each other, and as danger climbed their noses, their eyes, their ears, a dark warning. And suddenly they were two demons. But there was only one way out. Carried away by their momentum, the older one fell into the mud with his brother. It was a free-for-all down there! Endless seconds! Not one or the other ever got up. The back of the older one could be seen for a moment, but his head could not escape the marsh, and inevitably sank back into it.

The fight considered the most interesting is at night under the weak light of the moon. The pale moonlight makes it look phenomenal, and the expression and fury of the fighters changes dramatically; the dark makes them look ten times bigger, modesty and respect for humanity disappear with the light, especially if women are fighting.

While in the daytime cunning rage can hide, and is never demonic, not so at night when it purples or whitens a face immediately, fixing it in a hellish expression. It's a pity this expression can only be seen in half-light. Nevertheless, this moment the face is attacked is an unforgettable sight. No matter how furious the fight is, this one expression never changes. (The night is also good because it is serene, given up to a single passion.) These hideous grimaces sink their teeth into you, these expressions you may not see in a lifetime, and which always appear here, attracted by the night and the horrible circumstances. The spectators from upper class Hac society never fail to explain to you that it's not the combat that attracts them, but the revelations that come from each face. It's vital, of course, that the fighters be close relatives, or at least old enemies.

I found cities where nobody is ever at peace because their taste for certain spectacles is so strong. And the young people don't have the restraint of the old.

It's easy to introduce some wild beasts into a town (there are plenty of them on the outskirts). Suddenly, three or four black panthers come out of a traffic jam who, albeit distraught, know how to endure the most awful wounds. This is Spectacle Number 72. Oh! of course! the organizers of this entertainment planned it without any malice. But when you are on the street, it's better not to admire this spectacle; you should act quickly because the black panther thinks so fast, terribly fast, and it's not uncommon for a woman or a child to die from horrible wounds.

Of course, the authorities make a good-natured effort to suppress these distractions. "Young people try experiences that are a little brutal," they say, "but their hearts are in the right place. Besides, this spectacle pays the fine."

The fine is 25 bachs paid by each organizer. (All spectacles numbered above 60 pay the fine.)

While I was complaining about my house being robbed, somehow in broad daylight, not to mention it was next door to the office where I was (all the silverware was taken, and only one dish was left), the police captain said: "I'll follow procedure. But if there is one plate left, then this certainly is not a robbery, it is Spectacle Number 65. As the victim you will receive 50 bachs from the fine."

And a few moments later, a young man, like the kind you find in every country, came in and said: "Here's your silver," as if it was him who had the right to be annoyed.

"Not very smart of you," I said with contempt, "what did you get out of it?"

"280 bachs," he replied triumphantly, "all the balconies of the neighbors were rented."

After everything I still had to carry home, at my own expense, all my silverware.

They also have "Public Fire Companies." Large ones, smaller ones, they are situated on the shoulders of a boy.

If you look carefully enough, you will see some of them sneak into rich neighborhoods with baskets of fire.

Hey! Hey! It will be important to make a deal with these young people before the fire gets so big it attracts a crowd eager for drama, one that won't lift a finger to save your house.

Of course they won't. The crowds are crazy about fires.

Their specialty is animal fights. Every animal which has the slightest aptitude for fighting (and which ones don't?) is put under observation, studied, and experimented on in order to learn their hostility toward the hundreds of other species caged for this purpose. This continues until they have obtained fixed and repeatable reactions.

They've learned that all it takes is a tweak to the environment of an intelligent and gentle animal to fill it with unsustainable rage that, if matched with the right diet, can provoke the softest and most mushy soul. If their pharmacy is so vast, effective, and truly unique in the world, they owe it to the knowledge they've acquired from the preparations for these fights. I saw ferocious caterpillars and ear-splitting demon-canaries from which everyone fled in terror. (As you might expect, they also equip those animals nature left most naked with weapons and armor of all kinds to make them deadly.)

Often during the middle of the day, on one of the streets of the capital, you will come upon a man in chains, who looks happy, watched by a squad of Royal Guards. This man is being led to his death. He has just "attempted to kill the king." Not that he even had a reason to be unhappy! He only wanted to earn the right to be solemnly executed in a courtyard of the palace with the royal guards present. The king, needless to say, is not made aware of any of this. These executions haven't interested him for a long time. But the condemned man's family gains great honor, and as for the condemned man, after a sad life, one he probably messed up himself, he finally finds some happiness.

Every adult has the right to present Spectacle Number 30, which is called "Death in a Palace Courtyard," if they spontaneously confess afterwards that while "attempting to kill the king" they made it past the large gate, the gate to the small garden, and an entrance door. It isn't very difficult, as you can see, which is intentional, so that the people who have never known happiness have a way to find some.

The real difficulties would have begun at the second door.

Every year it is tradition for the Hacs to train a few child martyrs by making them suffer abuse and obvious injustices, by inventing motives and frustrating obstacles, all based on lies, in an atmosphere of terror and mystery.

The men chosen for this work are hard-hearted, brutish, and supervised by cruel and skillful leaders.

In this way they have trained great artists and poets, but also assassins, anarchists (we always have setbacks), and above all reformers, and hardliners.

When a change is made to the customs and social institutions, it is owing to them; if, in spite of their small army, the Hacs have nothing to fear, again they owe it to them; if, in their clear language lightning flashes of anger have been fixed, beside which the honeyed tricks of foreign writers seem boring, it is to them that they owe it, to a few raggedy, wretched, and desperate kids.

Moreover, for those who turn against these celebrities, there is always the Society for the *persecution of artists*.

That day they drowned the chief of staff and three cabinet members. The people were hysterical. The famine that lasted all winter had pushed them to extremes. I was afraid for a while that they would pillage our neighborhood, which is the richest. "No, no," I was told, "don't be afraid. This is obviously Spectacle Number 90, which will naturally be followed by 82 and 84, and the usual spectacles. But to be safe, we'll ask."

One person consulted his father, another his grandmother or a high ranking official. It was Number 90, after all. "But it's better you don't go out," they told me, "unless you have a few strong attack dogs because the bears and wolves, which are part of Number 76, will be released around four o'clock." The following week, as the situation worsened and still no one was doing anything about the famine, I felt the risk of seeing a few spectacles in the 80s was high. My friends found everything funny. But my unease was too strong, and so I left, perhaps forever, the land of the Hacs.

I told you words can't be trusted. Now you know numbers can't either. We can change the name of a thing but that won't make it any less the thing it is.

Number 76.

Bear bating.

What did Gertrude Stein say? "Pain is a pain is a pain is a pain."

Imagine wolves that have been made to starve let loose in a town where a hungry bear also roams. At least no one tied the bear to a stake by one leg like we did for hundreds of years in other countries. The Hacs have no Saint Francis to talk sense into the animals, by which I mean the humans. By which I mean us. As a species we have committed so many heinous crimes against nature and ourselves.

Most of us sit around and say how awful things are and hope they will get better, will get more decent, will get more humane. In the deepest center of our being, I believe we all want this. But the obstacle is hope, as Camus reminds us.

Hope is a shiny city on a hill where nothing happens. Apathy is the mayor and boredom is the creed. The ovens stay cold, and no one clucks in the roosts. In the city of hope there is no work and no rest. No phones ring, and no cars rumble down the street. No one cries and no one laughs, thus in the long and muted history of Hope, there has never been recorded on a single street the sound of that most divine of human expressions, the laugh-cry.

As much as I love stillness and peace and quiet, I don't want to live in a place with no laughter. Love is action. Hope is not. We have to love our way into the tomorrow that we most desperately want.

Was the man driving my taxi a woodchuck? I've heard one Vermonter refer to another Vermonter as a woodchuck. What on earth would make someone think of woodchucks when they see another person? Urban Dictionary tells us:

woodchuck

volunteer fire fighter

*Did you see those woodchucks saved another basement
  yesterday?*

woodchuck

upstate NY slang for a person of limited means; often on
  public assistance. The woodchuck is usually very crass and
  does not adhere to social norms.

Did you see those woodchucks? Two or four legged?

woodchuck

a person who lives far away from populated areas

That woodchuck does not come into town too often

woodchuck

a term used for a native Vermonter who displays Vermont
  characteristics. Derogatory if used by a person out of
  state, otherwise known as a flat-lander, or "out of stater"

*The flat-lander from out of state who cannot drive in snow
  called the maple-syrup-chugging logger who owns a farm
  and wears plaid a "woodchuck," as the woodchuck pulled the
  $50,000 SUV with a ski rack out from the ditch with his rusty
  tractor that he was driving down the highway*

woodchuck

a biology teacher at a high school who smokes "Jurassic
  Pot" and has substitutes play movies that are obsessed
  with earthquake safety

*According to Josiah Suxo, Miss Wanless is a woodchuck,
  vampire, and Dr. Evil*

woodchuck

common, ordinary, ignorant American. Usually asked
  questions by TV reporters in front of grocery stores,
  woodchucks respond with pat answers given to them by

Fox News. Woodchucks are overwhelmingly Republican and are a majority of the Tea Party.

TV REPORTER: *what do you think about Global Warming?*
WOODCHUCK: *There is no such thing. That's all a hippie Democratic conspiracy!*

woodchuck
term for a country person whose main job in life is to cut firewood to sell in the city or suburban areas. usually in a beat-up, four-wheel drive truck with high wooden sides to carry extra firewood. After cutting and splitting the wood they "chuck" it into the back of the truck. If driven by a female, this could be due to the fact that the male has lost his driver's license.
Looks like that woodchuck must be doing pretty good; he got a new woodchuck truck!

woodchucker
when you add definitions to urban dictionary without actually defining them.
Kyle added business plan *to Urban Dictionary but didn't actually define it. What a woodchucker.*

I could tell you that since its founding, this country has been obsessed with who belongs and who does not belong. And that labels help people feel they belong just as surely as they make others know they are not welcome. I bet someone smarter than me and with more time would tell you that the Toltecs and the Greeks and the Mongols and the Babylonians and the Aztecs and their like all invented their own labels to make clear who was one of them and who was not.

This is the language of empire.

In the hands of a person who fears losing their land and livelihood, language becomes a tool to preserve power, to maintain a status quo that guarantees when they lay their head to sleep at night that when they wake, the world will be just as they left it when the sun set. Who, having found happiness and security for their family, would not wish for the very same thing?

We all would, my son. I wish it for us after I lock the doors and set the alarm at nightfall. But this desire, this wish for regularity, comes at a steep cost. I am a child of empire just as you now are. And yet we battle daily for inclusion alongside our brothers and sisters who are seen as being of mixed descent. Just because we are sometimes seen as second-class citizens in our own land, a land that used to belong to the Spanish Empire before it was stolen from the Indigenous tribes, that doesn't mean our people haven't adopted the same obsession with color and its shades as the colonizer. Before you jump to judge our own people, remember that adopting the prejudices of those who say you now belong to them is one of the quickest ways to preserve your life.

Psychology calls this fawning.

It is like grasping for a root on the side of a cliff as you and your family are pitched over the side because you are seen as different and thus possessing no value.

Some days I wish we were woodchucks.

Not someone from Vermont or someone who sells wood or even a volunteer firefighter. No, I wish we were a family of groundhogs living our lives without worrying about the words other groundhogs would use to determine whether we fit in or not. Knowing a thing would be more important than naming it. We could even be rid of the words *father*, *mother*, *child*, *grandmother* and replace them all with *beloved*.

In this life there are those we love and those we do not. And the difference between them is less than we would ever care to admit.

TE AMO,

TU PAPA

Epilogue

I am a sick man . . . I am a good man. An attractive man even. Once the handsomeness of my own reflection so took me by surprise that I had to wink and blow myself a kiss. I have sought to learn everything about my sicknesses, so much so that I fear I know too much sometimes about what it is that hurts me. I follow all of the treatments my doctor commands.

I meant to say doctors.

I've collected them like snowflakes since you were born that one winter years ago. There is the general one who speaks Spanish like us; the knee doctor; the throat butterfly doctor; the doctor of the skin; the one for the guts; the ear, nose, and throat one; the hip doctor; and the head doctor. People used to call that last one a shrink. She was the one who said I have postpartum depression.

People call it a disease of the mind, but I know it is really a sickness of the heart.

And why shouldn't I have become heartsick, when two weeks after your birth, I flew on a plane back to New Jersey where I lived with my shadow in my burrow, counting the days until I would emerge once a month to see you again? At the time I was the world's only known burrow dweller capable of flight.

Week after week, winter slowly gave way to spring.

Outside my burrow magnolias and daffodils and cherry trees splashed their paint everywhere. Squirrels crawled among the crocuses, and I took it all as a cruel mockery because my burrow was empty.

When you were two and said, "This pickle is like a cucumber, isn't it?" I thought the earth shook above me as if it had been struck by the hammer of creation.

One day shots were fired on campus while I was teaching. A groundhog was acting strangely, they said. How many people who look like us have been arrested or shot because someone thought we were "acting strangely"? We would need a lot more fingers and toes than we were given at birth to count them all.

A white policeman from town came and shot the poor groundhog before he found out that you tend to act strangely when a red-tailed hawk has savaged you. I walked by that groundhog's burrow every day, so when I learned about the killing, I thought of you and immediately wrote the school. I told them she probably had kits deep in her burrow, and who would see to them before a fox or starvation paid a visit?

I lied about myself when I said I was a good man. I thought if I wrote the words, then maybe it might become true. But no, I never was, though I have tried, even mightily once or twice.

If I was a good man, I would have done more than asked after those chubby chucklings lost their mama. Son House sang that "love is a worried old heart disease." That disease can make a burrow out of a heart, so when I finally left New Jersey for good a few months later, I had a burrow that traveled within me whose tunnels and rooms grew when the pandemic came and the virus settled inside your abuela. She became sick and then better, then sick and better again for good. A new job came so that I could see you and your mama and sister almost every day, but still I could not see my shadow, so I wandered in a fog from room to room underground.

Have we ever talked about how sometimes I teach premed students how to tell stories of sickness? One time I asked them to write a script for an actor who would pretend to be sick. I wrote one too, and it looked something like this.

SCRIPT EXAMPLE

Name: Tomás Q. Morín

Age: 45

Chief Complaint: "I feel depressed and like if I die, then it might be better for everyone. I don't want to be a burden."

Identifying Data: College-educated professor; workload stressful at times; partner, children, good home life.

Scenario: Your postpartum depression began three years ago after the birth of your son. Your last major depressive episode was over twenty years ago when you were a graduate student. At that time you were also diagnosed with obsessive-compulsive disorder and dysthymia. You consider yourself an optimist but have been unable to experience hope.

Patient Profile: Concerned/anxious about this problem. You lean to one side during the interview. Sitting is uncomfortable because your psoas muscle is clenched from chronic stress, and you have developed early osteoarthritis in your hips. Talk in a low voice but louder than a whisper. Make infrequent eye contact and keep your hands together in front of you. If asked to lie down, close your eyes and appear as if you could sleep forever.

History of Present Illness

When did it start? *3 years ago.*

How did it come on? *It gradually started over 7–10 days, on and off.*

Did you have any injury to bring this on? *Yes, leaving my son.*

How frequent is the pain? *Almost daily.*

How long does it last? *I feel as if there is no end.*

Where is the pain? *The heart and the head. The heart-head or the head-heart.*

If probed further: *Currently have back and knee pain together but can have knee swelling without knee pain.*

Describe the pain. *Sharp.*

How bad is the pain? *On a scale from 1 to 10 (10 being the worst), it ranges from 2–4; now it's at 5.* Does it interfere with your life? *After an hour driving, I get stiff. Haven't been able to do my usual exercise. Can't bend over to pick things up. House-work is painful (like doing laundry). Lifting my son is painful.*

Relieving factors? *Massage therapy.*

Aggravating factors? *Exercise, standing, bending over, and stress.*

Back/leg pain during pregnancy? *Not applicable.*

Any other symptoms beside pain? *Fatigue, trouble sleeping, lack of energy, melancholy.*

Past Medical History

Answer NO to the following: *Tobacco, intravenous or recreational drugs.*

Medications? *Multivitamin, pig pills, and vitamin D3.*

Alcohol? *Socially, a few cocktails a month.*

Hospitalizations? *None.*

Exercise? *I usually play basketball, lift weights, and walk.*

Script covers all problems/abnormalities. If asked about any other problems, everything is normal.

Family History

Mother is living; one sibling—a younger brother; father had six other children. History of anxiety, laughter, thyroiditis, love, cancer, gentleness in mother's family.

Questions to Ask

This heart is like a brain, isn't it?
This body is like a life, isn't it?

I never thought I could be more visible until X-rays and MRIs looked deep inside of me, beyond the skin others could not see past. Doctor visit after doctor visit, diagnosis after diagnosis, treatment after treatment, all attempts to remedy my underlying condition, chronic inflammation.

I am a man afire.

There are many like me who walk this earth like a burning bush with nothing to say. I don't know how others survive, but I can tell you my secret. Remember when Camus returns to Tipasa and says, "In the depths of winter, I finally learned that within me there lay an invincible summer"? The memory of those summers of his youth spent in the ruins bathed in the light and sound and smell of the sea was a shield for him.

What I have come to know, my son, is that in the depths of fire, within me there lies an invincible winter.

One spreads within you too, O child of cold who crawled into the heart of winter.

Don't let the fools deceive you into thinking that summer is good and winter is bad. The seasons slip out of the cheap clothes of morality we would dress them in. Saint Jimmy reminded us that "God gave Noah the rainbow sign, No more water, the fire next time!" Well, the fire is here, and it is all around us.

While people throw themselves into the flames in panic, let the frozen tundra that spreads within keep you still. In that silence that most would find brutal but that you and I crave, the white bear sniffs the air for the slick seal and the fox and the hare and the snort of the reindeer. The sound of their blood travels for miles like a drum across that beautiful and uncluttered open expanse.

Once, when I ventured out on a –40-degree day, the skin of my forehead grew sluggish, and my nose hair froze within seconds. I had never felt quite so close to death as that sunny day, which is to say I had never felt quite so close to life.

While the new century makes others dance on the hot coals of their convictions, we will walk our shaggy souls out onto the ice and cut a hole to the watery burrow below whose gentle darkness promises to feed us.

We will say nothing.

We will let love have the last word.

Acknowledgments

My thanks to the communities at Rice University, Vermont College of Fine Arts, and Drew University for their support. A very special thanks to the Office of Research and to the School of Humanities of Rice University for their support of this book with a Creative Ventures grant.

Heartfelt thanks to my rockstar agent, Dan Mandel, for believing in this book.

Eternal gratitude to my editor Courtney Ochsner for helping me bring another book into the world.

I couldn't have written this book without the support of friends who held the light for me as I stumbled through my dark night of the soul: Courtney Zoffness, Sunil Yapa, Erin Evans, Hasanthika Sirisena, C. Dale Young, Vievee Francis, Jessica Smith, Marcus Burke, Rowan Buckton, Laura Lee Huttenbach, Josh Lopez, Curtis Bauer, Twister Marquiss, Katie Kapurch, and Jill Patterson.

Much love and hugs to Rebecca, Chloe, and Jack, my family whose love expanded my idea of what I thought family could be beyond my wildest imaginings. When all is said and done, I am now from the beautiful country of love and kindness we built together.